THE DOG IN ART FROM ROCOCO TO POST·MODERNISM

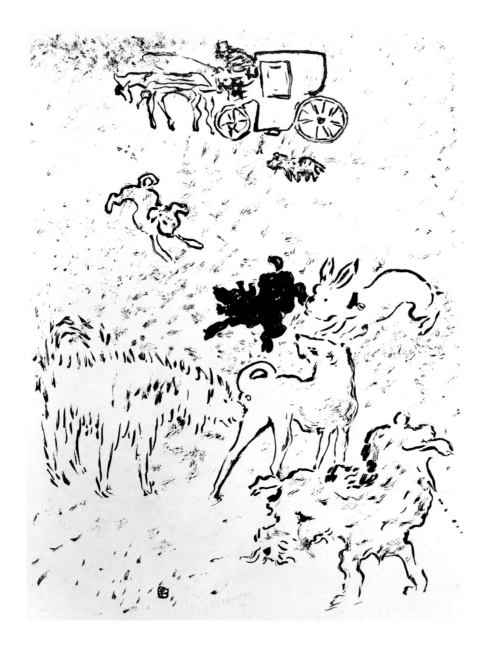

THE DOG IN ART
FROM ROCOCO TO
POST·MODERNISM

ROBERT ROSENBLUM

HARRY N. ABRAMS, INC. · PUBLISHERS

Editor: Ruth A. Peltason
Designer: Elissa Ichiyasu
Picture Editor: J. Susan Sherman

Library of Congress Cataloging-in Publication Data
Rosenblum, Robert.
The dog in art from rococo to post-modernism / by Robert Rosenblum.
p.   cm.
ISBN   0–8109–1143–4
1. Art, Modern.   2. Dogs in art.   I. Title.
N7668.D6R67 1988
704.9′432—dc19   88–1400

To HARRY, MOLLY, *and* LOLA,
the international set,
and to CLARA, *a true New Yorker*
—welcome weekenders!

CONTENTS

PREFACE

The dog in art? For an art historian like myself who has spent most of his time writing about epic movements (Romanticism, Cubism) or major artists (Ingres, Picasso, Stella), some explanation is in order. Concerned with the Romantic Movement as the foundation of those fundamental attitudes toward art, life, and feeling that are still with us today, I long ago thought about approaching this overwhelming revolution in terms of isolating particular themes—children, Gothic architecture, military heroes, natural disasters, among others—and considering how the depiction of these subjects changed. One of these themes was the animal, and I was amazed to discover that the drastically new interpretations of both wild and domestic beasts in the years from c. 1760 to c. 1840 contained virtually a microcosm of the revisions of form and emotion familiar to that period. Thanks to the accident of an unsolicited commission to write a very short piece on paintings of dogs for *Architectural Digest* (July 1986, pp. 86–90), I was for the moment obliged to put the animal kingdom into much narrower focus, and quickly realized that no animal could tell the story of modern art and culture better than the dog. Horses, of course, could speak volumes, too, but from the mid-nineteenth century on, they slowly became remote from human experience as mechanized means of war, transport, and agriculture rendered them obso-

9

lete. And even compared to cats, dogs have always occupied positions in the animal world that were closest to the affections of human beings, whether as participants in the hunt, as loyal companions in wild nature or on a farm, or as sustaining personal comforts in the richest and poorest of city and country dwellings. After all, who but a dog could have deserved the kind of commemoration achieved by Hachiko? The pet of a professor at the University of Tokyo, Hachiko, an Akita, would go to greet his master at the Shibuya subway station every day. When the professor died, Hachiko waited for him until midnight, and then returned home alone, an act of devotion he repeated for nine years until his own death in 1934, after which his admirers, in Japan and abroad, collected funds to erect a statue of this noble animal at the station exit.

For of all animals, dogs continue to play roles that mirror most closely the activities and needs of the humans they live with. Indeed, many of the canonic masterpieces of modern art include dogs who seem essential to the meaning of the human cast of characters. Who can forget the insouciant mongrel standing with its head turned away from the grave in Courbet's *A Burial at Ornans*; or the juxtaposition of a roaming stray and a confined and pampered pug in front of Seurat's *A Sunday at the Grande-Jatte*; or the sinister silhouette of a black dog almost camouflaged beneath the table in the New York version of Picasso's *Three Musicians*? But to think of these works is also to realize that the scope of the topic is daunting, and that some restrictions had to be made to balance the motif at hand with the surprising proliferation of examples. Finally, I decided to limit myself to works that focused on dogs alone, permitting people to appear, if at all, only in secondary roles (at the invisible upper end of a leash; as a sleeping infant; as

an inert amputee). But even within these limitations, it turned out, I believe, that the story of dogs from the eighteenth century to the present, and therefore within the evolution of our own cultural cycle, could be told consecutively and in a revealing form. From these changing attitudes toward the world of canines, it was possible to confront directly a remarkable number of major issues in our heritage: the welling sentimentality of early Romanticism and its popularization from the Victorian era right into the world of Walt Disney; the Marxist awareness of the definition of and conflicts between nineteenth-century social classes; the mechanization of all living things, whether human or animal; the Freudian pursuit of those irrational, animal instincts that presumably control us humans; the post-Hiroshima horror of sentient solitude in an apocalyptic void; the ironic excavation of the art-historical past associated with our present Post-Modernist condition. In all these grand domains of our cultural history, dogs, when experienced and recorded by human beings who are also artists, play essential parts.

In compiling this three-part essay, I have had the most diverse and welcome range of help from both art historians and dog lovers, often one and the same person. An article that provided a model for me in its combination of scrupulous art-historical research with an effort to interpret the meaning of dogs in a particular time and place is Richard Thomson's " 'Les Quat' Pattes: the image of the dog in late nineteenth-century French art" (*Art History*, vol. 5, no. 3, September 1982, pp. 323–37). Important for me, too, in both specific and broad ways, were three exhibition catalogues: *J.-B. Oudry* (by Hal Opperman), Fort Worth, Kimbell Art Museum, 1983; *Sir Edwin Landseer* (by Richard Ormond and Joseph Rishel), Philadelphia Museum of Art, 1981;

Dogs! (by Lynne Warren), Chicago, Museum of Contemporary Art, 1983. And the publications of The Dog Museum of America (in New York until 1987, but now in St. Louis) also helped me to get my bearings on the subject. For clues to the widest range of studies concerning dogs in everything from Greek mythology and Rembrandt to Shakespeare and botanical classification, see Robert Baldwin, "A Bibliography of Dogs in the Humanities" (*The Journal of the Delta Society* vol. 2, no. 1, winter 1985, pp. 6–13).

Inevitably, I owe a debt to all those friends who called my attention to this or that work which might be a candidate for inclusion in these pages. Of these, Charles Stuckey was particularly enthusiastic and supportive with ideas and art-historical data. Here, my major regret is that, given the restrictions to a book in these modest dimensions, so many works had to be excluded—dogs by such famous artists as Antoine-Louis Barye, Berthe Morisot, or Pierre Alechinsky; by such specialists in dog painting as Roy de Forest and Donald Roller Wilson; or by such unexpected amateur artists as Prince Albert. That there were so many candidates for illustration here was a tribute to the surprising abundance and importance of the theme.

The support I received in the actual making of this book also demands special gratitude. Susan Sherman patiently and efficiently tracked down photographs not only from major museums but from the most obscure private collections, and Elissa Ichiyasu fused these illustrations and my text into a book whose design elegantly mixes the contemporary and the historical aspects of the 250 years surveyed here.

Lastly, I should like to thank my editor, Ruth Peltason, who not only first proposed the idea of expanding my interest in this subject into a book, but who, like the subject, remained loyal and steadfast and who, like the author, was both smiling and serious about the whole project.

Robert Rosenblum
New York, January 1988

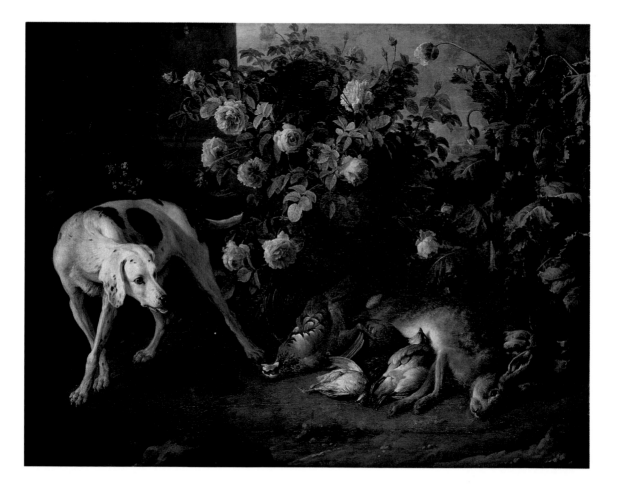

1. Alexandre-François Desportes

DOG WATCHING OVER GAME BESIDE ROSEBUSH

1724. Oil on canvas, 42⅛ × 52″. The Louvre, Paris

· I ·

FROM ROCOCO TO
ROMANTICISM

When an animal has feelings that are delicate and refined,
and when they can be further perfected by education,
then it becomes worthy of joining human society.
To the highest degree the dog has all these inner qualities
that merit human attention.

Comte de Buffon, HISTOIRE NATURELLE, *vol. 5 (Paris, 1755)*

As man's and woman's best friend (and at times, worst enemy), the dog has played every imaginable role in the theater of Western life and art. Susceptible to almost any interpretation by the human species with whom they learned to live, dogs, even in the ancient world, could be perceived in wildly unlike ways. The Egyptians, for instance, could sanctify and worship them, personifying Sirius as the ever-faithful dog-star, since every year it benevolently signaled with its appearance the flooding of the Nile and the need to move the cattle to higher land. And when the family dog died in Egypt, the human survivors, at least according to Herodotus, all shaved themselves as a symbol of deep mourning.

The Hebrews, however, could vilify dogs, associating them with forbidden unclean animals and with pagan idolatry, so that even today, Chassidic Jews find dogs repugnant intruders in human society. In the post-classical world, the extremes of deifying or abominating dogs were tempered by more terrestrial and practical attitudes, in which dogs could be integrated into human life not only as workers who played a major part in the hunting of animals for sport or food, but as loving, loyal, and unselfish companions who gave to their masters and mistresses far more than they demanded in return. In a Christian context, dogs, esteemed already in the ancient world for their fidelity, could become an earthly emblem of that virtue, carved in postures of steadfast watchfulness alongside many tomb effigies or, in the most unforgettable example, Jan van Eyck's *Arnolfini Wedding Portrait*, symbolizing, in the form of a cuddly lapdog, not only marital fidelity but, as has also been suggested, erotic desire, equally appropriate to the commemoration of a marriage.

It was not, however, until the eighteenth century, when so many inherited molds began to crack, that we may begin to recognize the birth of our own modern sensibilities toward dogs or, as a matter of fact, toward everything else. The history of art, after all, tells us not only about art with a capital A, but about the history of ourselves. Made by men and women living in particular times and places, art mirrors, sometimes directly, sometimes subliminally, almost every change of human experience through history. And since nothing is irrelevant to understanding that history, whether the curriculum of a rural school in eighteenth-century England or the train schedules of late nineteenth-century France, the role of dogs, in life as in art, might possibly tell us almost as much about what happened to the Western world over the last two centuries as the recounting of great wars and revolutions.

Our story may begin with the most privileged domain of the early eighteenth century, that of the French monarchy, and with a glimpse of the most privileged dogs within it, those who accompanied the king and his court on the royal hunt. Descendants, it would seem, of the goddess Diana's hunting dogs, these animals—dachshunds, spaniels, greyhounds, pointers—commanded sufficient attention, affection, and respect to be given individual names, both classically noble (Polydore, Pompée) and charmingly colloquial (Petite Fille, Coco), as well as

to have their portraits painted individually and in beautifully choreographed packs. Of the many artists employed in these tasks, none was so illustrious and productive as the long-lived Alexandre-François Desportes (1661–1743). Born into rural poverty, he got to Paris by the age of twelve, became a court painter in Poland, and then, in 1696, returned to France where Louis XIV quickly named him the official painter of the royal hunt, which the artist actively observed on horseback. Accepted into the Academy, housed in the Louvre, pensioned by the king, he even spread his fame and art to England, which welcomed his elegant depictions of its own favorite sport. And he outlived his first Bourbon employer, continuing to paint the royal hunt for the regent, and then for another obsessive huntsman, Louis XV. In a typical canvas, one dated 1724, we have an intimate view of what might be thought of as the archetypal Rococo hunting dog *(fig. 1)*. Far less ferocious or robust than his seventeenth-century ancestors, this animal, apparently observed from life, takes a watchful pose over the fruits of his royal profession's labor. Nature is here, to be sure, in the profusion of flora and fauna on the soil; but artifice triumphs throughout. A column base at the left regally frames this cornucopian bounty, which the dog dutifully guards with the light-footed grace of a dancer. Strewn before us with the casual elegance of the most chic of Parisian butcher displays, the dead game— quail, grouse, hare—offer a mouth-watering preview of royal dinners to come. And a royal table setting is equally suggested by the animated bower of pink roses and leafy bushes that grow with luxurious abundance over the bodies of what we feel are the still-warm spoils of the hunt. Clearly, a royal gardener is also at hand.

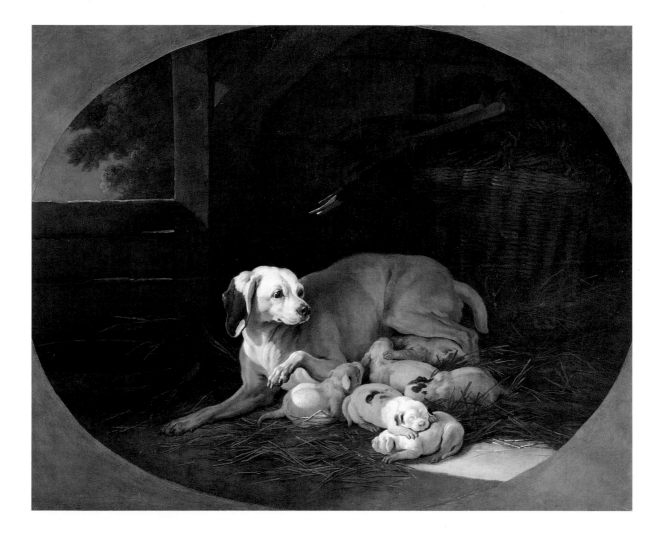

2. Jean-Baptiste Oudry

BITCH HOUND NURSING HER PUPPIES

1752 (Salon of 1753). Oil on canvas, 40¾ × 52″. Musée de la Chasse et de la Nature, France

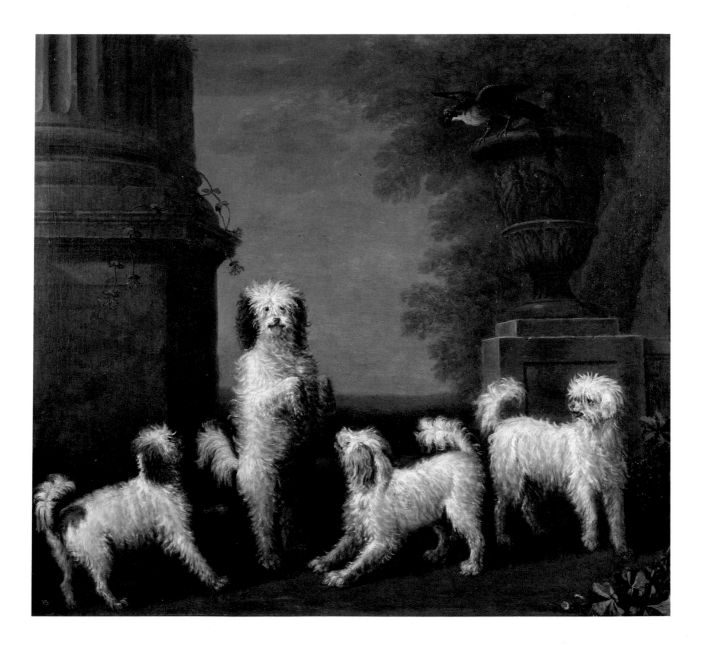

3. John Wootton

THE DANCING DOGS

1759. Oil on canvas, 44 × 54″. Wallington House, The National Trust, Northumberland, England

As heirs to the great eighteenth-century revolutions, we all know that Desportes's confection of a dog at work for the then fourteen-year-old Louis XV and his court was doomed to disappear by the end of the century, to be replaced, slowly but inevitably, by other dogs, other masters and mistresses, and other emotions that we may gradually intuit as belonging to our own modern traditions. And already within the early eighteenth-century territory staked out by artists who were chiefly concerned with depicting the hunting dogs of Louis XV, a pivotal change took place at the Paris Salon of 1753. There, the aging court painter, Jean-Baptiste Oudry (1686–1755), who had spent most of his life recording the royal hunts, exhibited a modest, but as it turned out, sensational painting that suddenly turned from the named, aristocratic working dog, employed by the king and the nobility, to an anonymous mother in a stable, with a brand-new litter of six puppies. The official two-part description in the Salon catalogue was *Chienne allaitant ses petits. Ce groupe est éclairé par le soleil* (*Bitch hound nursing her puppies. This group is illuminated by the sun*). These two points warranted immediate response *(fig. 2)*.

Although the eighteenth century had inherited Descartes's rationalist belief that animals, not having souls, were only mechanistic creatures, automatons with no more capacity for feeling than a cuckoo clock, this philosophical belief in an absolute separation of humans from animals became harder and harder to maintain in view of the evidence provided by, among other things, the maternal devotion of a dog or a cat or the intelligence of a toy poodle who could learn circus tricks. In 1755, the great naturalist the Comte de Buffon, who also worked for Louis XV as supervisor of the royal menagerie, was able to discuss in his multi-volumed *Histoire naturelle* the way in which dogs, by virtue of their proximity to us as creatures capable of being educated and of displaying a wide range of emotions, could properly function in human society. His opinions clearly were shared more and more by the Western world from the mid-century on. For spectators at the 1753 Salon, Oudry's female hound became a paragon of devotion, and she was often referred to as "the mother," as if she had usurped the human role familiar in images of Christian maternity and contemporary mothers and children, a kind of canine Caritas. This ascent from animal dumbness to sentient virtue and tender feeling was in good part a product of Oudry's intense focus on the mother's alert and protective expression as well as on the cuddly innocence of her nursing and snoozing brood, who offer kennel equivalents of pudgy Christian angels or classical putti. It is also underlined, as the title proclaimed, by the dramatic luminary effects, which Oudry's contemporaries recognized as rivaling those in a famous Rembrandt now in the Louvre, a Holy Family in a lowly carpenter's shop where sunbeams also enter the darkness through a window and cast a supernatural glow upon the archetypal scene of humble Christian maternity. Appearing at the Salon in the company of such subjects as the *Death of Socrates* and the *Delivery of the Keys to St. Peter*, Oudry's painting, which the Baron von Grimm found the best of the show and which the artist himself apparently considered his finest work, obviously struck deep new chords of sensibility that permitted humans to project their most heartfelt emotions into an animal kingdom.

Oudry was to die shortly afterward, in 1755, but his painting, of which he was to make in 1754 a second variant with only two puppies, was posthumously re-exhibited in engraved form at the Salon of

1759, by which time the welling sentimentality of this icon to motherhood had more fully permeated art and life. In France, it was soon to be the decade of Jean-Baptiste Greuze, who in the 1760s had begun to venerate, in terms of genre painting, the ineffable joys of motherhood as well as the irresistible equation that could be made between the sweet innocence of puppies and of children. And it was also to be the decade in which, on both the enlightened sides of the Channel, in the novels of Samuel Richardson and in the writings of Jean-Jacques Rousseau about childhood and education, the idea of breast-feeding as something positive and good rather than as something relegated only to the animal world and to the lower classes who could not afford wet nurses would begin to take hold. Even French and British nobility, as depicted by Greuze and Reynolds, would consider being eternalized in paint as affectionately nursing their own children in an abandon to nature with a capital N, thereby recapturing the buried instinct unearthed in Oudry's image. It may be no surprise that Oudry's nursing dog was to be singled out for positive comment by Greuze's most enthusiastic supporter, Diderot, in his critique of the 1767 Salon; but it is surprising to realize that this presumably unambitious painting, the swan song of one of Louis XV's court artists, may well have pinpointed the moment when that all-embracing empathy between man and dog was first recorded so fully and so tenderly in a canine environment where we, the spectators, are the only human intruders.

Oudry's choice here of natural instinct over man-made artifice was precocious. As often as not, mid-eighteenth-century painting continued to mirror dogs as Rococo marionettes, performing elegantly for human delectation, or in the role of lapdogs, as comforting personal cushions, who, however,

might begin to share human confidences. As for dogs as spectacle, there is a typical British country house performance recorded by John Wootton (1682–1764), a painter of Oudry's generation who, like most eighteenth-century British sporting painters, specialized in portraits of the dogs and horses owned by his wealthy patrons. His *Dancing Dogs* of 1759 *(fig. 3)*, probably executed for Sir Walter Calverley Blackett, the owner of Wallington where it still hangs, is, in effect, a bit of private theater or, better said, circus, in which the four dogs, suitable more for play than for work in the hunt, go through their paces stiffly, but with would-be balletic grace. The familiar convention of British portraiture in which the figure is enframed by a large column base or stone urn here creates a mock stage space for the performers as well as dwarfing them to an amusingly minuscule scale. Their breed, related to the modern Bichon Frise, was particularly fashionable in France; and judging from the names inscribed beneath this quartet—Lusette, Madore, Rosette, and Mouche—Sir Walter's dogs were probably luxury imports from across the Channel.

It was in France, in fact, that the Rococo dog par excellence was cultivated and depicted. In any contest for the perfect example, a small canvas, dated 1768, by Jean-Jacques Bachelier (1724–1806) might be a prizewinner *(fig. 4)*. A painter of exotic animals that ranged from a Polish bear and an African lion to a Chinese pheasant, Bachelier already in 1765 had painted a poodle reputed to be the pet of the ten-year-old Marie Antoinette. In this later work, a so-called 'dog of the Havannah breed' performs like an enchanting wind-up toy, begging, from pink hair ribbon to perfectly manicured nails, for the spectator's attention. Prophesying the Romantic breakdown of a world measured exclusively

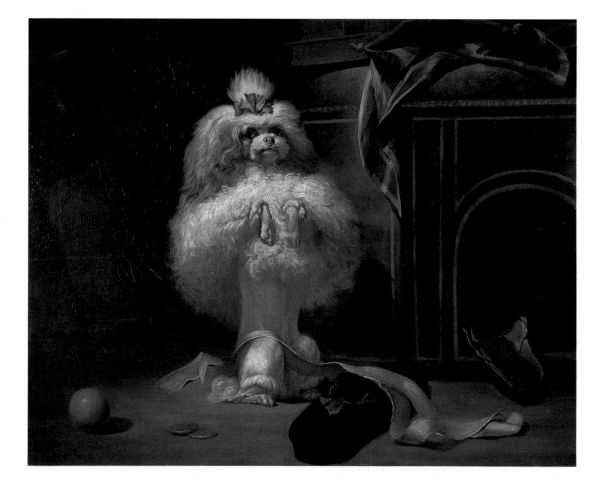

4. Jean-Jacques Bachelier

DOG OF THE HAVANNAH BREED

1768. Oil on canvas, 28¼ × 34½″. Bowes Museum, Barnard Castle, Durham, England

by human scale, we see this domestic corner through, so to say, a dog's-eye view. A canine Lilliputian, the poodle, even when sitting up, is smaller than the books that lean at the left; and the ball, coins, and slippers that litter the floor in front of the doghouse seem to belong to a race of giants this pampered court jester entertains.

Such miniaturist scale, familiar as well in the many diminutive porcelain dogs of the Rococo period, could even be translated into marble, as in the carved dogs of the highly eccentric British sculptress, Anne Seymour Damer (1749–1828). A strong-willed woman of great classical erudition

whom contemporaries observed stalking about the countryside dressed in male attire, she was a close friend of the brilliant writer and socialite Horace Walpole. Although her range of subjects extended to such remote antique personages as Apollo, Isis, Coriolanus, and Augustus Caesar, as well as to such contemporary ones as George III, Lord Nelson, and Charles James Fox, she was no less renowned for her marble animals. Displayed at the annual Royal Academy exhibition in 1784, her *Two Sleeping Dogs (fig. 5)* must have provided an adorably relaxed moment within the company of England's most aspiring artists, from Reynolds to West. But in fact,

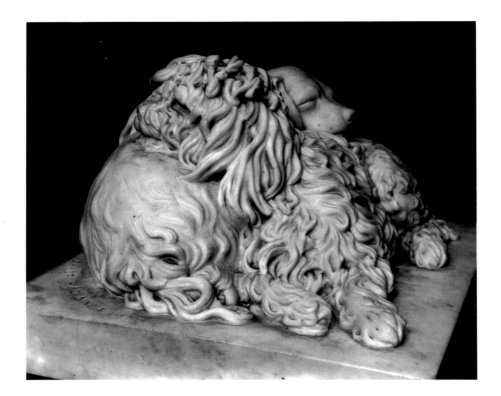

5. Anne Seymour Damer
TWO SLEEPING DOGS
Royal Academy, 1784. Marble, 15½ × 12″. The Duke of Richmond and Gordon at Goodwood

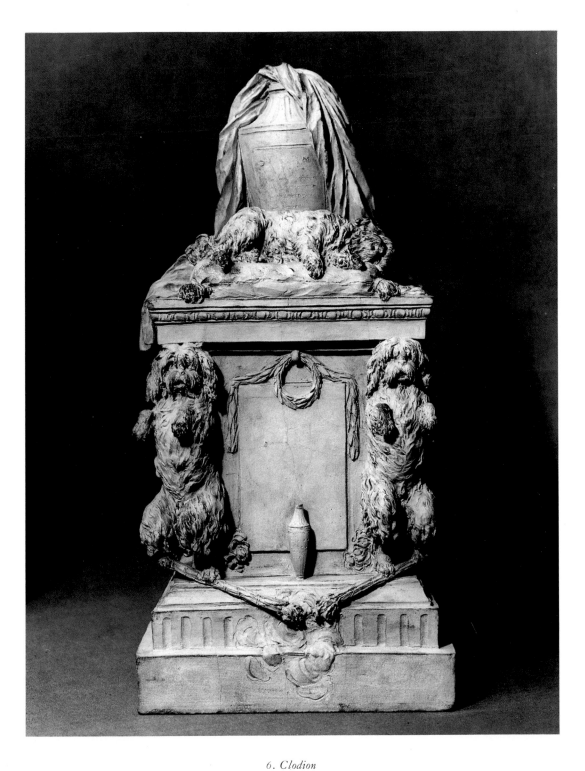

6. Clodion

MAUSOLEUM FOR NINETTE

c. 1780–85. Terra-cotta, height 14¾″. Musée Historique Lorrain, Nancy

Damer shared the academy's loftiest pretensions, for the inscription she carved on this little marble is in Greek, translatable as ANNE DAMER OF LONDON MADE IT. But such matters aside, the work still appears a tour de force of miniaturist carving, a shaggy mound of marble fur in which we can hardly separate one lapdog from the other. Before this virtuosity, we may almost justify her friend Walpole's extravagant comment that Damer would be considered a prodigy in Italy since she modeled like Bernini. Widowed as a young and beautiful noblewoman, Damer carried her fiercely independent sense of full identity with a predominantly male profession all the way to the grave. In her will, she requested that the tools of her calling—mallet, chisel, apron—be buried with her, as well as the ashes of her favorite dog.

Had Damer carved her own dog's gravestone (and in the late eighteenth century, many dogs and other pets began to be buried, as so many still are today, under monuments conceived in the image of their masters' and mistresses' tombs), it might well have resembled a terra-cotta mausoleum designed in France in the 1780s by the textbook exemplar of a Rococo sculptor, Claude Michel (1738–1814), always known as Clodion *(fig. 6)*. An exact contemporary of Fragonard's, Clodion, too, was a virtuoso master whose vibrant touch and dollhouse scale could explore every pleasurable variation on the theme of the soft flesh of young women and the furry coat of those ubiquitous lapdogs who shared their mistresses' amorous adventures at the dressing table or in the bedroom. Clodion's funerary monument, which, like Damer's *Sleeping Dogs*, is only a bit over a foot in height, was probably never intended as a model for a real monument, but only as an amusing

mock-serious bibelot that mimicked the exalted allegories of eighteenth-century tombs. Above, the deceased Ninette lies on the kind of cushion she undoubtedly enjoyed in life, echoing the mournfully drooping rhythms of the drapery that shrouds the crowning urn. Below, two other lapdogs sit up and beg in the guise of caryatids supporting a tomb, while their hind paws hold, in the manner of funerary genii, smoking torches. Such artifice, adapted to human erudition and wit, removed the canine race as far from its inherent reality as did the familiar Rococo images by artists like Boucher of infants who, instead of playing, are engrossed in such serious professions as architecture or astronomy.

It was the kind of artifice that could also turn dogs into the most elegant of still-life objects, as in a painting of the late 1770s by Anne Vallayer-Coster (1744–1818), *Les Petits Favoris (fig. 7)*. Elected to the Royal Academy of Painting at the early age of twenty-six, Vallayer-Coster rapidly made an official and also a public reputation for herself as a still-life painter in the tradition of Chardin, but one who preferred to move from his more humble fare to such luxury items as pineapples, alabaster and lapis lazuli vases, lobsters, and plovers. It is hardly a surprise that when, on a rare occasion, she turned to dogs, they should fit comfortably into this category of the most expensive, pre-Revolutionary sensibilities. Here, three cosseted and beribboned pets—a pair of sleepy King Charles spaniel puppies (the painted equivalent of Damer's carved dogs) and a lean, highstrung Italian greyhound—are arranged, together with a dog collar, upon a tasseled velvet cushion, as if they were the most precious of artifacts. The somber, bare background (an austere nod backward to

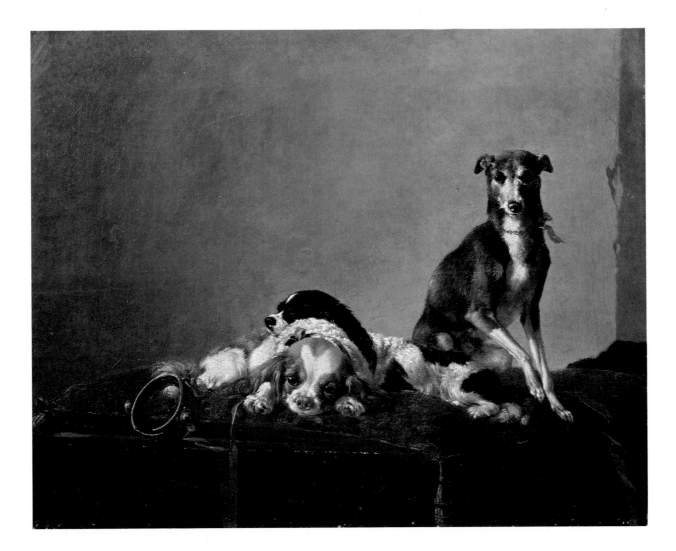

7. Anne Vallayer-Coster

LES PETITS FAVORIS

c. 1775–80. Oil on canvas, 16¹¹⁄₁₆ × 20⁹⁄₁₆″. Collection John and Laura Pomerantz

Chardin's more low-keyed, serious ambience) only intensifies by contrast the pampered refinement of this trio who, in canine terms, almost make us feel the inevitability of the Revolution which annihilated Vallayer-Coster's most enthusiastic patroness, Marie-Antoinette herself, whose portrait the artist had painted in 1780, probably close to the time she was completing *Les Petits Favoris*.

Confronted with the transformation of dogs into creatures we feel would expire instantly were they placed back in nature, we may cry, as many other eighteenth-century artists did, for an antidote. The clearest of these voices was that of the century's greatest animal painter, George Stubbs (1724–1806), who ironically shared the exact life span of the master of the toy poodle, Bachelier. As author and illustrator of ambitious treatises on zoology and comparative anatomy, Stubbs brought a scientific empiricism to his observation of the widest range of animals, from such exotic newcomers to the British Isles as a cheetah from India presented to George III or a kangaroo from Captain Cook's expeditions to the most familiar of those British domestic animals assimilated into human society, dogs and horses. His dog portraits—no other word will do to suggest their high degree of psychological and physiognomical individualization—include many breeds, from water spaniels and spitzes to foxhounds and poodles. As for the latter, Stubbs, in his *White Poodle in a Punt*, probably dated c. 1780 *(fig. 8)*, offers the perfect counter-statement to the Rococo poodle by insisting on a record of truth, instinct, and nature, regressive and purifying abstractions that eighteenth-century reformers in all domains would invoke as new, therapeutic ideals for art, for people, and for society. As always, Stubbs seized first the sheer physical facts of the animal, scrutinizing it with the precision and objectivity of the scientist he was. But his accurate vision embodied new emotions as well. The dog is seen, as it were, on its own turf, undiminished by the scale of the human beings who would have accompanied it on a hunt. Alone and dominating a space as ample and noble as that usually accorded a horse and rider, the poodle is still shown partly within a manmade context, for it floats on a punt. But remarkably, Stubbs examines not only the outer appearance of the dog, whom we feel we could spot immediately in real life, but its inner, psychological nature as well. For its head, rather than being seen in a neutral profile view, as in the case of Stubbs's depiction of emotionally less interesting creatures, a rhinoceros or a zebra, turns to confront the spectator with a disturbed and disturbing gaze. We intuit that the animal, its four feet resting on a floating boat rather than on secure soil, is anxious about its temporary helplessness. And as a strangely sentient backdrop in nature, Stubbs has silhouetted the poodle against that most emotive of trees, the weeping willow, whose increasing presence in the gardens and paintings of the late eighteenth century would often provide a resonant corollary in landscape for melancholy or introspective human feelings.

We may glimmer as well these new inflections (which, for want of a better word, we still call Romanticism) in the animal paintings of the famous British portraitist Thomas Gainsborough (1727–1788), whose pictorial fluency and dash (the very opposite of Stubbs's painstaking and stable clarity) have often made critics align him with French Rococo style. Judging by the fact that Gainsborough's first signed and dated picture (1745) was of a bullterrier named Bumper seen alone and alert in the woods, it was to be expected that there would be further explorations into the private lives of dogs. Such was the case in an extraordinary canine maternity of the late 1770s with an equally odd commission *(fig. 9)*. Himself musically talented, Gainsborough befriended two illustrious German musicians in London, Johann Christian Bach and Karl Friedrich Abel, who composed and played music at the court of Queen Charlotte. Moreover, he painted both their portraits. That of Abel includes his two cherished possessions, the viola da gamba which he played as a royal chamber musician, and his pet Pomeranian, a Prussian breed then relatively new in England. But the dog's portrait was soon to rival her master's; for Gainsborough then arranged for Abel to give him viola da gamba lessons in exchange for a portrait of the Pomeranian and her new puppy. Proudly but stealthily guarding her only infant, who is protectively shadowed beneath a clump of wild morning glories in a darkening woods, the Pomeranian confronts us not as a lower member of a human social structure but as a sentient creature at home in a totally natural environment, like a lioness in front of her cave. Far more remote from human habitation and scale than Oudry's barnyard mother *(fig. 2)*, she seems to change before our eyes from an adored and diminutive human lapdog to a wild animal whose commanding size dominates the picture from upper to lower edge, much as it controls that part of the forest she has staked out as her own.

For the late eighteenth century, such excursions into a totally natural world were constantly balanced by an imaginary, ideal realm, more noble, more heroic, more dramatic than the here and now of ordinary human or animal life. Often, the over-

whelming imprint of classical antiquity could transport a theme into remote, legendary realms, even within the unlikely category of a design for a doghouse as envisioned by the greatest British architect of his generation, Sir John Soane (1751–1837). Receiving from the King a three-year traveling fellowship, Soane spent three years (1778–80) in Italy, where he met a major patron of Neoclassic art, Frederick Hervey (Bishop of Derry and 4th Earl of Bristol), with whom he visited the classical ruins around Naples. On Christmas Day 1778, they visited what was left of a Roman villa, and wondering where the dog kennels were, the bishop suggested that the young Soane design one in the classical style for his country seat at Downhill, in Northern Ireland. Soane quickly obliged with a pair of large architectural drawings for a "Canine Residence," for which one was in a more practical sober style, and the other *(fig. 10)* in a personal echo of the most megalomaniac French architectural fantasies of the generation of Peyre, Ledoux, and Boullée. The reverse side of the Rococo's diminutive scale, this archeological extravaganza, which mixes everything from the stumpy Greek Doric order Soane saw at Paestum to the high dome of the Pantheon, suggests a building of such sublime dimensions that even the clouds appear to float below rather than above the crowning sculpture of a pack of sky-bound hounds. At the entrance, awesome in its vista of the grandiose symmetry of a distant, classical civilization, a pair of sculptured dogs guard, like lions, the canine precinct. Within this sanctuary, we see the only living specimens in this dream of antique splendor, two dogs who drink from one of the fountains that circle the gigantic kennel. As extreme a fantasy as Clodion's tiny mausoleum *(fig. 6)*, Soane's classical

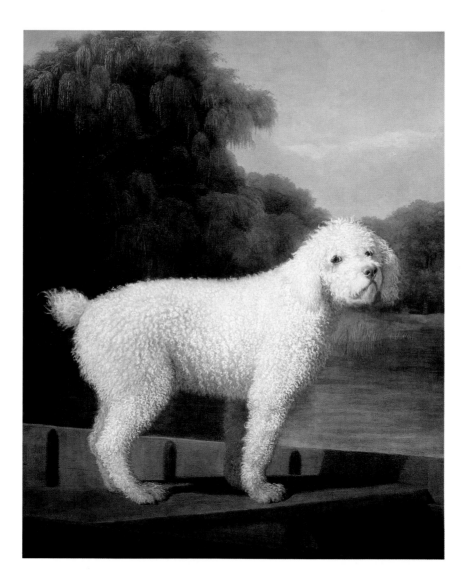

8. George Stubbs

WHITE POODLE IN A PUNT

c. 1780. Oil on canvas, 50 × 40″. Paul Mellon Collection, Upperville, Virginia

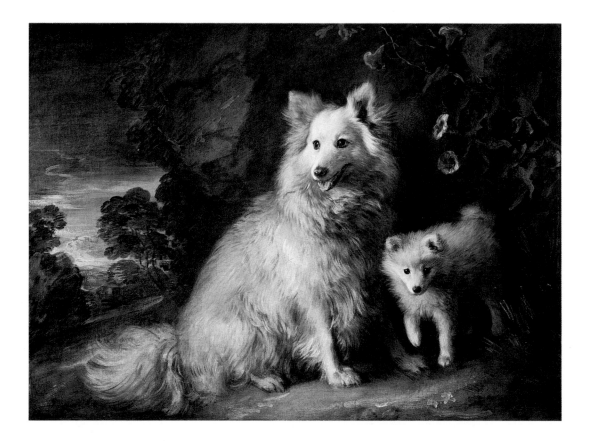

9. Thomas Gainsborough

POMERANIAN BITCH AND PUPPY

c. 1777. Oil on canvas, 32½ × 43½″. The Tate Gallery, London

vision also remained unexecuted, leaving us only a drawn record of the probably tongue-in-cheek drama provided by the problem of adapting a lowly functional building in the British Isles to the most wildly ambitious reconstruction of the "glory that was Greece and Rome."

Infinitely more modest, but also saturated with classical allusions, was a small canvas shown at the Paris Salon of 1801 by Mme Jeanne-Elisabeth Chaudet (1767–1832), a member of that generation which fell under the spell of the great Jacques-Louis David. The subject of this painting *(fig. 11)*, being something of a private invention, needed to be explicated by a long title in the Salon catalogue: *An infant sleeping in a crib under the watch of a courageous dog which has just killed an enormous viper.* Mme Chaudet specialized in sentimental or dramatic genre scenes that frequently involved dogs and children, conjuring up, for example, such improbable narratives as a young girl teaching her dog to read (1799 Salon) or a young girl lunching with her dog and insisting that it say grace (1812 Salon); but her style, her references, and sometimes even her overtly classical subjects evoked the more high-minded and learned aspects of antiquity that inspired so much art at the turn of the century. In this case, the dog itself is the noble hero, risking its life to save its sleeping, helpless ward in a manner that parallels the human

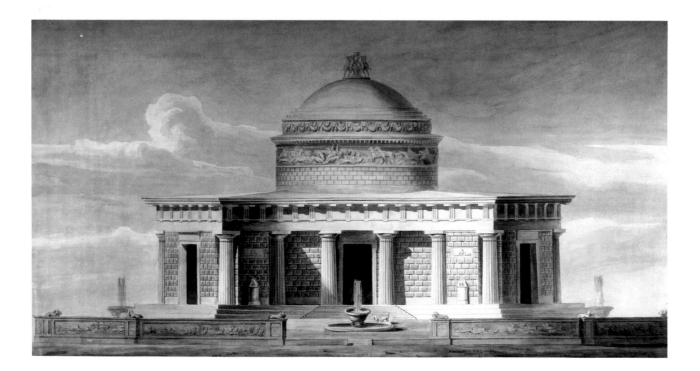

10. Sir John Soane

DESIGN FOR A CANINE RESIDENCE

Rome. 1779. Redrawn by C. J. Richardson, c. 1835. Sir John Soane's Museum, London.

sacrifices for state or family so abundant in the classi-cizing dramas of David and his school. The Greco-Roman aura of this uncommon stoicism is further amplified not only by the planar, friezelike con-struction of the painting, which echoes, in a minor key, the funerary dramas of the Davidian world, but by other antique resonances as well. The peacefully sleeping infant, for instance, recalls in its perfection of pumiced surface and scant but harmonious drap-eries a polished antique marble, such as Ariadne or, more to the point, the Sleeping Cupid, whereas the conjunction of infant, dog, and conquered viper again conjures up classical sources, here inverting the tale of the infant Hercules, who demonstrated his precocious prowess by strangling snakes while dogs, in some depictions of the tale, would cringe terrified. But finally, all these erudite reverber-ations (a mark of ambition at the Paris Salon) are subsumed by the straightforward image of the archetypal Fido, who, in so many nineteenth-cen-tury paintings to come, would continue to guard the human species with uncommon displays of courage.

Like the human beings, remote or contemporary, who were increasingly venerated in an era of Revo-lutionary heroism and soaring genius, dogs in the late eighteenth and early nineteenth century could scale the most Olympian heights. None is more memorable as a record of achievement than that por-trayed in a painting listed as *Portrait of an Extraordi-nary Musical Dog (fig. 12)*, when exhibited in London in 1805 at the Royal Academy. The artist, Philip Reinagle (1749–1833), specialized in animal painting, ranging from more prosaic dog portraits, such as *Major, a celebrated greyhound* (exhibited in 1805 together with this musical prodigy), to a mon-strous battle between a vulture and a hyena over a captive hare (his diploma piece). It is known that Reinagle was particularly interested in the degree to which spaniels could be trained, so it is likely that this musician was one of his exceptional students. However, no record of this spaniel's public fame seems to have been found as yet in the London news-papers of the day, and the painting may only mirror, we assume in highly idealized form, Reinagle's pri-vate aspirations, which may have been as imaginary as the music notation on the open score. But whether true or false as a document of a canine prodigy, Reinagle's painting unforgettably records the extrav-agant extremes of empathy that could be projected upon dogs and other animals by the turn of the cen-tury. Recalling the precocity of the child Mozart at the piano, but moving more into the dramatic do-main of the archetypal alienated genius, Beethoven, the spaniel fixes its gaze upon us with the riveting intensity of Romantic passion. And given the per-former's isolation in a domestic corner, with only a landscape view through an open window for com-panionship, we sense not the performance world of Rococo toy poodles, but a lonely, introspective terri-tory of private reverie. Were the sun to set, we could find no better score for this "extraordinary musical dog" to play than the *Moonlight Sonata*, composed in 1801, only four years earlier.

The close-up, eye-to-eye confrontation with Rein-agle's spaniel was a familiar formula in Romantic portraits of people, and perhaps reached fever pitch in the work of Théodore Géricault (1791–1824), as in his acutely individualized depictions of patients suffering from a variety of mental illnesses. It was Géricault, in fact, who could transform, with ut-

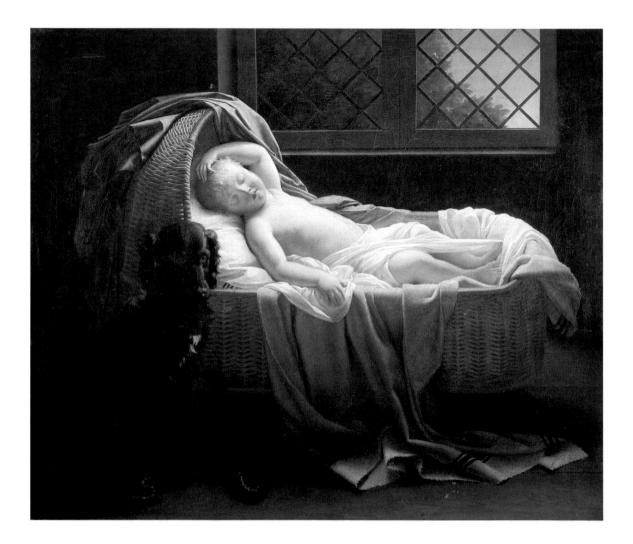

11. Jeanne-Elisabeth Chaudet

AN INFANT SLEEPING IN A CRIB UNDER THE WATCH OF
A COURAGEOUS DOG WHICH HAS JUST KILLED AN ENORMOUS VIPER

Salon of 1801. Oil on canvas, 44⅞ × 52¾″. Musée des Beaux-Arts, Rochefort-sur-Mer

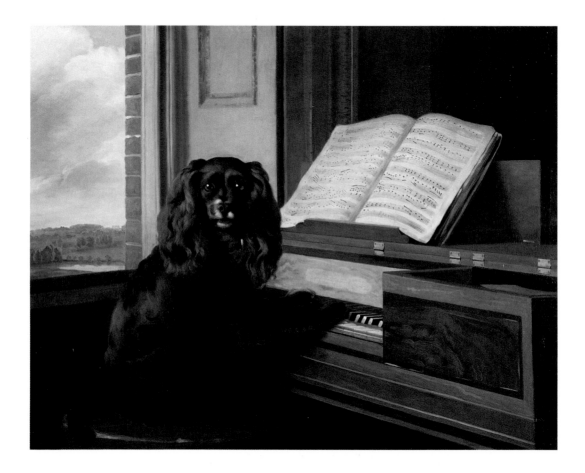

12. Philip Reinagle

PORTRAIT OF AN EXTRAORDINARY MUSICAL DOG

Royal Academy, 1805. Oil on canvas, 28¼ × 36½″. Virginia Museum of Fine Arts, Richmond. Paul Mellon Collection

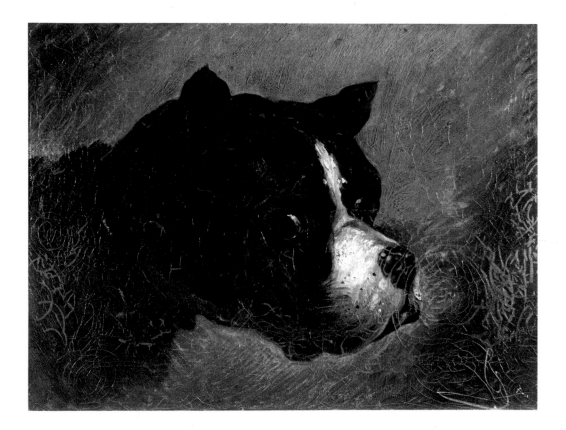

13. Théodore Géricault

BULLDOG

c. 1815. Oil on canvas, 16⅛ × 11⅜″. Musée des Beaux-Arts André Malraux, Le Havre

most vigor and persuasiveness, the passions of human psychology into those of animals, especially horses, whose expressions in his work match the most turbulent human spectrum of feeling. And on one occasion, probably about 1815, he painted a no less intense portrait of a bulldog *(fig. 13)*, which, despite its small dimensions, imposes its presence on the viewer as fully and dramatically as do Géricault's human sitters. A reflection of France's and Géricault's renewed and welling Anglophilia after the fall of Napoleon, the subject is an English bulldog (for which the French word, *le bouledogue*, is itself an Anglicization), and as depicted here, the animal is personified so fully that we feel we are meeting it on uncomfortably equal terms. It is its expression, not its body, that confronts us, its stocky head, with no background to deflect our attention, totally filling the canvas and its darting eyes meeting and returning our gaze. Together with Géricault's intimate but full-blooded encounters with the eyes and emotions of horses and people, this seemingly casual record of what was probably a friend's dog can hold its own in any gallery of Romantic portraiture, a penetrating glimpse into the unruly territory of animal emotions that can be shared by spectators who dare to look, and a probing that destroys totally the Rococo vision of dogs as adorable puppets manipulated by human hands. Fittingly, a lithograph of Géricault's bulldog was exhibited at the Salon of 1824 in what was to become a memorial tribute to the artist, who had died prematurely only months before.

In Romantic England, this exploration of canine drama also accelerated, at times to melodramatic heights, as was often the case in the work of the long-lived James Ward (1769–1859). His portrait of a poodle named *Buff*, signed and dated 1812 *(fig. 14)*, is an act of Romantic animal liberation, in which this artificially trimmed pet, with its pompon tail and restraining collar, is set free in total isolation upon a remote precipice overlooking an agitated sea and a horizon of infinite expanse. Were the dog a human player, he might well be cast in the role of Byron's Manfred standing on the Jungfrau (a literary product of the same decade as Ward's painting) or of such precocious Romantic themes as Gray's *Bard*, whose hero similarly confronts his lonely destiny in a sublime landscape of breathtaking mountain views. Ward's poodle, his eyes staring theatrically into the abyss, his ears swept back by the wind, his legs assuming an agitated but steadfast stance, is the very image of a Byronic hero. Indeed, Buff was almost that, having accompanied his master, Lieutenant Colonel Chestmaster, to Spain during the Peninsular War. Now, back home near the cliffs of Dover, Buff faces the Continent, recalling, one imagines, his Napoleonic adventures.

Given the emotional kinship with their masters and mistresses, dogs could rapidly become surrogate human beings, mirroring the belief of the great French naturalist Baron Georges Cuvier (1769–1832), that the dog represented the most total conquest the human species had ever made over the animal world, exemplifying every kind of courage and loyalty elicited for no other motives than those of gratitude and love. It was a point clearly made in Mme Chaudet's painting of a dog that had risked its own life to save that of a human infant, and it was a point that could support most of the work of the most famous dog and animal painter of the nineteenth century. Sir Edwin Landseer (1802–1873) was not only that, but the best known British artist of his generation, and one whose international fame was awarded with a state funeral and a tomb in St. Paul's

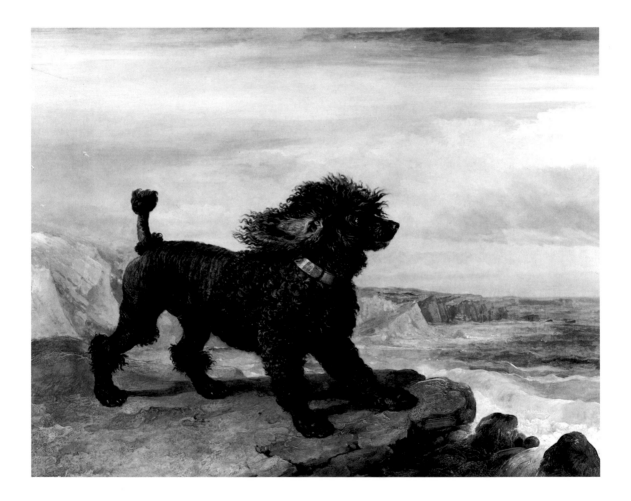

Cathedral next to those of Reynolds, Lawrence, and Turner. Landseer's name was to become synonymous with a Victorian sensibility toward animals. He was, after all, the official court painter for Queen Victoria and Prince Albert, depicting not only them but many of their royal pets, from macaws, lovebirds, and marmosets to greyhounds, terriers, and spaniels; and especially in his later works, dogs present a Dickensian panorama of nineteenth-century society, playing such roles as pompous judges, aristocratic sitters posing for their portraits, or beggars looking for crumbs under a rich man's table. But Landseer was also the product of a full-blooded Romantic generation, and his early work, in particular, is marked by a robust drama often set in malevolent nature, as in a scene inspired by a poem by Sir Walter Scott (whose pet dogs Landseer also painted) in which we see a faithful terrier who has remained for three months by the corpse of his master, the victim of an accident in a cataclysmic mountain setting.

The counterpart to such uncommon fidelity, in the face of natural hardships, was uncommon courage, as demonstrated in a painting Landseer exhibited at the Royal Academy in 1824. That year, coincidentally, marked the foundation of the Royal Society for the Prevention of Cruelty to Animals, which signified the official recognition, welling in the eighteenth century, that animals had feelings different from our own only in degree rather than in kind. The painting was titled *A Portrait of Neptune, the Property of William Ellis Gosling, Esq. (fig. 15)*, and confronted the spectator with a huge Newfoundland who amplifies to still more heroic dimensions the Byronic situation of Ward's *Buff* of the previous decade *(fig. 14)*.

The Newfoundland was a relatively new breed in England, and one whose impressive size and heroism made it immediately popular. Byron himself owned a Newfoundland named Boatswain, and after the animal died in 1808, not only wrote a poem commemorating its loyalty, but even had constructed on his own property at Newstead Abbey a funerary monument for his pet in which he himself also wished to be buried. At home in water, as Neptune's classical name suggests, the breed was famous for saving victims of drowning; and indeed, the engraving after Landseer's portrait of another Newfoundland, Bashaw, was titled *Off to the Rescue*. Here, Neptune seems to be standing at the ready, alert to any distress signals that might come from the tiny fishermen and their boats which, unlike the Newfoundland, are dwarfed by the breathtaking vista of rugged but treacherous sea, rock, and sky. By presenting Neptune as a paragon of courage, willing to risk his own life to rescue his human friends from a malevolent, storm-tossed sea, Landseer has virtually made the dog usurp the role of Romantic hero. It was a point further underlined in the title of a later portrait of a Newfoundland by Landseer, *A Distinguished Member of the Humane Society*, a reference to the organization founded in London in 1774 for the propagation of first-aid techniques to resuscitate the casualties of maritime disasters, a cause of death as commonplace in the early nineteenth century as automobile accidents are today. So potent were the artist's icons of Newfoundlands that the black-and-white variety he depicted came to be called a "Landseer."

Even Landseer's tributes to this breed, however, seem modest next to a three-dimensional one offered by the sculptor Matthew Cotes Wyatt (1777–1862),

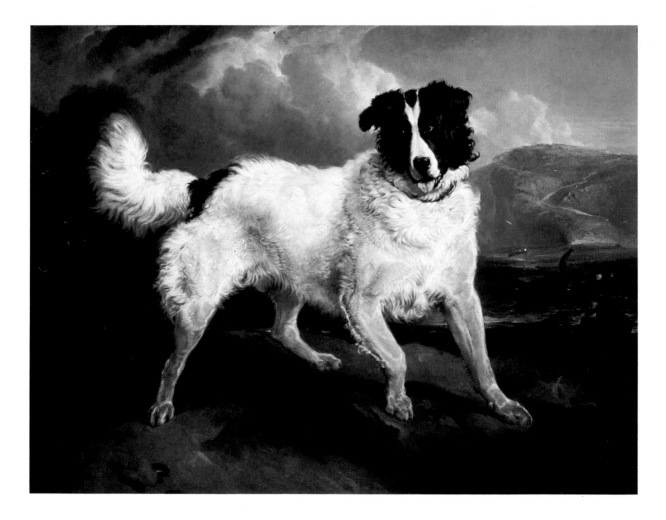

15. Sir Edwin Landseer

A PORTRAIT OF NEPTUNE, THE PROPERTY OF

WILLIAM ELLIS GOSLING, ESQ.

Royal Academy, 1824. Oil on canvas, 60 × 79″. On loan to the Philadelphia Museum of Art

whose official range of monumental sculpture in-cluded portraits of George III, Nelson, the Duke of Wellington, and the Duchess of Rutland. But it also included a commission from Lord Dudley in 1831 to eternalize his favorite Newfoundland, Bashaw, in what must be close to a lifesize replication (35 inches high) of the dog. It was only in 1834, sadly after Lord Dudley's own death, that Wyatt completed this sculpture, which was described in a catalogue of his works that year as "the most elaborate of a quadru-ped ever produced by ancient or modern art" *(fig. 16)*. Indeed, it may have been. Not only do gems simulate Bashaw's lustrous eyes, but the pri-mary material is a lavish polychrome marble, rang-ing from the yellow of the cushion on which the dog stands, to the blacks, grays, and whites that describe the irregular markings on his fur. But more re-markable still, Bashaw is transformed into an allego-ry; for like Mme Chaudet's dog of 1801 *(fig. 11)*, he tramples a snake. This bronze serpent, in fact, was in part a pragmatic addition, intended to secure support of Bashaw's weighty marble belly, but it could quickly escalate the meaning to the height of the title given to the sculpture when it was seen at the Crystal Palace Exhibition of 1851, *The Faithful Friend of Man Trampling Underfoot His Most Insid-ious Enemy.* Perhaps this inflation to lofty allegory would have satisfied the critic of the Royal Academy Exhibition of 1803, who complained at the vanity and littleness of those patrons responsible for the abundance there not only of mindless portraits of themselves, but of their favorite dogs, cats, and horses; but perhaps it might equally explain John Ruskin's later vilifying of Wyatt's sculpture in 1871 as an "iota of Miscreation," and as "the most perfect-ly and roundly ill-done thing which . . . I ever saw

produced in art." For Ruskin, at least, this preten-tious aggrandizement of a pet dog was offensively ludicrous.

But the allegorical treatment of dogs was hardly restricted to the excessive veneration of personal pets, and dogs as anonymous symbols reflecting hu-man situations could be explored by even such great Romantic artists as Runge, Goya, and Turner. As for Philipp Otto Runge (1777–1810), renowned for grandly ambitious and cryptic religious fantasies that would use the closest observation of nature for their abstruse messages, a lone dog may come as a surprise, though characteristically, it conveys an idea. Especially in the early years of his short life, Runge practiced the then common art of silhouettes, which were most often used around 1800 for render-ing profile portraits. But he also essayed other sub-jects with scissors and paper, including that of a common, folkloric parable of foolishness, a dog who, like an infant, tries to contact the moon by reach or by sound *(fig. 17)*. In this pristine and di-minutive cutout, probably executed in the late 1790s, Runge creates, in playing-card size and within the sparest, most linear vocabulary, a strangely haunting opposition between terrestrial desire and skyborne inaccessibility. Reminiscent of the white-on-blue cameo reliefs on Wedgwood por-celain, which were inspired, in turn, by Greek red-figured vases and their classicizing revivals in John Flaxman's outline illustrations (which Runge greeted enthusiastically), the earth-bound dog is as abstractly profiled and immaterial as the weightless rectangular plinth upon which it sits. Fixed on a field of pure, celestial blue, it is engaged in an eter-nal, allegorical dialogue with the Romantic full moon above, a circle whose geometric perfection is

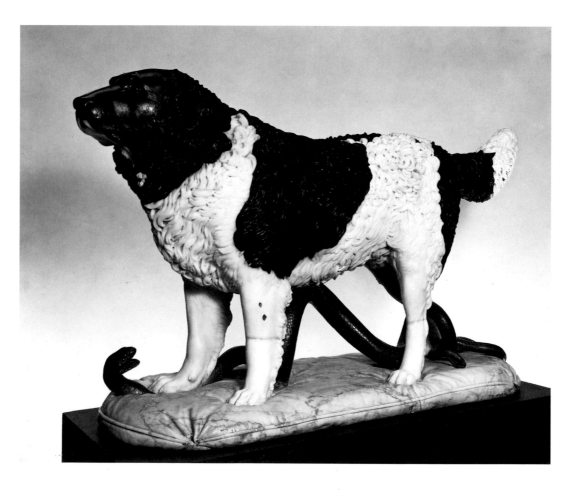

16. Matthew Cotes Wyatt

BASHAW

1831–34. Marble and bronze, height 35″ (without base). Victoria and Albert Museum, London

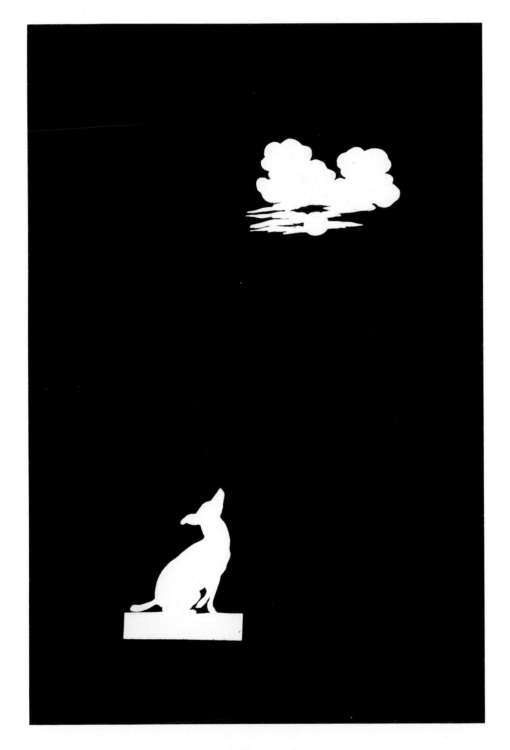

17. Philipp Otto Runge

DOG BARKING AT THE MOON

c. 1800. Paper cutout, 7⅛ × 4⅝″. Kunsthalle, Hamburg

18. Francisco de Goya y Lucientes

A DOG

1820–23. Mural transferred to canvas, 53½ × 32″. The Prado, Madrid

obscured by passing clouds in the night sky. Unimportant as it was within the swelling cosmological goals of Runge's art and thought, this minor work, in its compellingly succinct clarity and mystery, is indelible, looking forward to Miró's far more famous, and comparably incisive reincarnation of the same proverb-like theme *(fig. 44)*.

The enchanting isolation of Runge's dog, however, reaches tragic, indeed apocalyptic dimensions in works by Goya and Turner. As court painter to a long and rapidly changing succession of Spanish rulers, Francisco de Goya y Lucientes (1746–1828) had inevitably painted many aristocratic pets, whether a duchess's pug or poodle or a king's hunting dog, animals who clearly took their subordinate place in a human hierarchy. But as this ordered, rational world appeared to Goya to be collapsing around him, both under its own monarchs and the Napoleonic invaders, so too did it vanish in his later art.

In the notorious "black paintings," executed between 1820 and 1823 for his small farmhouse in the Madrid suburbs, Goya totally unleashed his most irrational fantasies in a series of cryptic, but interrelated paintings of his own invention and probably for his own eyes only. Of this often nightmarish sequence of images of a benighted, brutalized world, dominated by the darkest forces of sadism, desperation, and loneliness, none is so enigmatic, none so definitive a contradiction of the Age of Enlightenment as the tall vertical canvas simply titled, for want of a more explicit explanation, *A Dog (fig. 18)*. In it, we see only the grayish head of this solitary animal looking up toward a shadowy presence, perhaps the ghost of a vanished human master, in a hallucinatory landscape that seems to have dissolved earth, rock, sky into a dully luminous haze in which

neither man nor beast can find its bearing. For twentieth-century spectators, this horrendous vision of a last living survivor, dog not man, and one that seems to be struggling and sinking, perhaps into quicksand, can even conjure up after-images of nuclear disaster. For Goya, it must have meant a comparable extinction of any semblance of human reason and control. For all the erudite explanations that have been offered to help decipher Goya's image—it has been suggested that it alludes to everything from political allegories of restricted liberty to Renaissance allegories of the soul's ascension—such intellectual associations evaporate before the terrifying fact of this helpless, half-buried animal alone in a pulverized landscape. It was Goya's unique genius, but also the soaring imagination of the early nineteenth-century Romantics, that permitted something as pathetically ordinary as a stray dog to bear the crushing allegorical weight of an annihilated civilization.

Uniquely disturbing and original as Goya's canvas is, it can almost meet its match in a late watercolor by another great Romantic of a much younger generation, Joseph Mallord William Turner (1775–1851). In this small but unforgettable sheet, probably dating from the early 1840s, the traditional title, *Dawn after the Wreck*, would suggest an explanatory scenario *(fig. 19)*. Against a red-tinged sky in which the sliver of a crescent moon can still be seen, the invading light of dawn silhouettes a wraith of a dog, presumably the lone survivor of a shipwreck. In desperation, it barks toward the sea, seeking human companionship or mourning its drowned master.

Turner's greatest champion, John Ruskin, who so hated Wyatt's *Bashaw*, found this watercolor one of

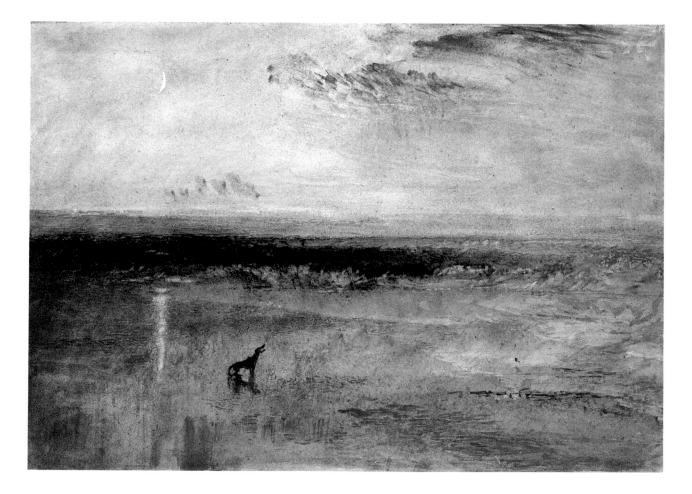

19. J. M. W. Turner

DAWN AFTER THE WRECK

c. 1841. Preliminary drawing in pencil; watercolor with brush, red chalk, rubbing and retinting on white paper.
Courtauld Institute Galleries, Sir Stephen Courtauld Collection, London

the artist's saddest and most tender works, describing the dog as "utterly exhausted, its limbs failing under it, and sinking into the sand . . . howling and shivering." For him, as perhaps still for us, this barren scene evoked an epic tragedy. Indeed, as in Goya's painting, we are confronted with a malevolent environment, untamable by the laws of perspective or navigation, where man can no longer endure.

Next to the cheering popular heroism of Bashaw and other Victorian Newfoundlands ready, at the water's edge, to save foundering mankind, Turner and Goya strike the most pessimistic chords, resounding in the apocalyptic reaches of the Romantic imagination. Not until the years of the Second World War would artists again be able to transform a lone dog into a poignant symbol of human desolation.

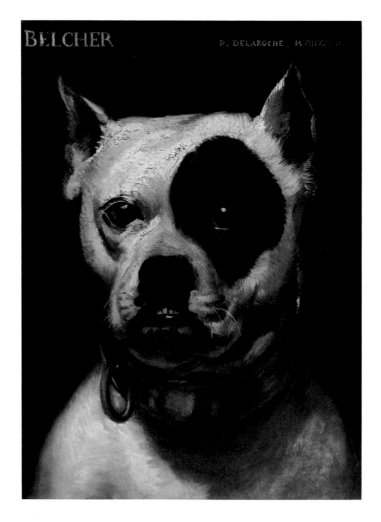

20. Paul Delaroche

PORTRAIT OF BELCHER, AN ENGLISH BULLDOG

1832. Oil on panel, 12½ × 8¹⁵⁄₁₆″. Private collection, New York

· II ·

FROM REALISM TO
FIN · DE · SIÈCLE

[In Paris] the stray dog happily frequents other members
of his race who have been reduced to slavery. He even
seems to prefer them as playmates and above all as victims of
his love. Perhaps he takes a malicious pleasure in soiling
their beautiful combed, shined, washed, and perfumed fur,
and sowing his seed in the midst of respectable families.

Jean Richepin, L E   P A V É   *(Paris, 1883)*

Although Turner could transform fact into dreamlike fiction until his death, well into the Victorian age, in 1851, younger nineteenth-century generations insisted more and more on the here-and-now truths of the prosaic, material world. In canine terms, this might mean, for one, the depiction of dogs as reflections of those ever more mobile and collisive economic levels, from desperately impoverished peasants to well-heeled urban industrialists, which provoked mid-century thinkers like Carlyle and Marx to examine the problems of class struggle and to propose solutions. (By the 1850s, in fact, the confrontation of, say, stray mongrels and pampered whippets or pugs on the streets of London and Paris would become a familiar symbol of the jostling social frictions of burgeoning cities.) And it could also mean a boom in dog portraiture, with plain and fancy records of favorite city or country dogs who, like their masters and mistresses, would be photographed or painted by a growing industry of portraitists.

A new counter-Romantic tone can already be sensed in the portrait of a French count's English bulldog, Belcher, who in 1832 sat for one of the top establishment artists of the July Monarchy, Paul Delaroche (1797–1856) *(fig. 20)*. Although at the

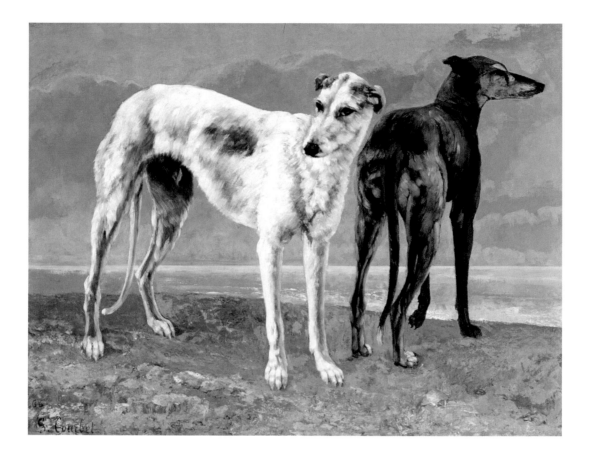

21. Gustave Courbet

THE GREYHOUNDS OF THE COMTE DE CHOISEUL

1866. Oil on canvas, 35 × 45¾″. The Saint Louis Art Museum. Gift of Mrs. Mark C. Steinberg

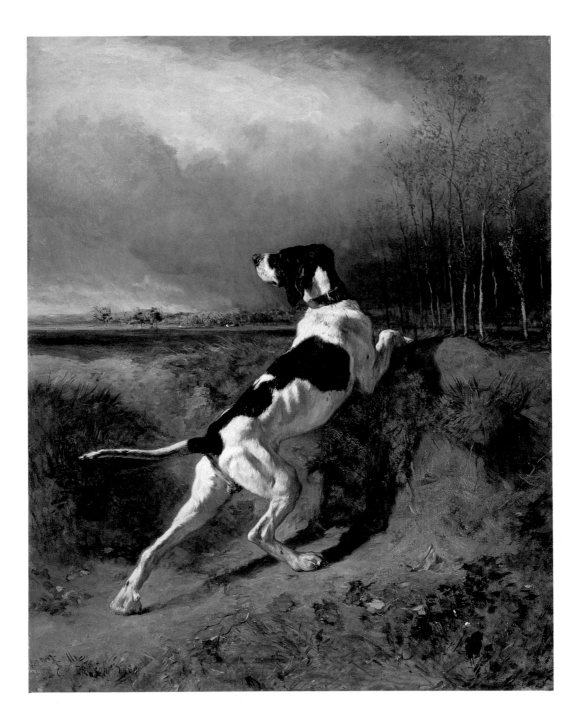

22. Constant Troyon

HOUND POINTING

1860. Oil on canvas, 64 × 51½". The Museum of Fine Arts, Boston. Gift of Mrs. Louise A. Frothingham

time concerned primarily with what appear to be, even before Daguerre's invention of 1839, meticulously photographic reconstructions of such dramatic moments in English history as the execution of Lady Jane Grey or the imminent murder of Edward IV's children, Delaroche could also pause for an aristocrat's commission to record a favorite English bulldog, whose breed, like the artist's subjects, reflected the Anglophilia then rampant in France. Almost a direct descendant, one feels, of Géricault's earlier bulldog of c. 1815 *(fig. 13)*, *Belcher* nevertheless proposes a new world of dog portraiture. In place of the Romantic artist's disconcerting confrontation with an uncollared, anonymous dog that suddenly turns to the spectator with a wide-eyed animal stare, *Belcher* is an image of propriety and restraint. Beneath his name, inscribed in imitation of the pre-Revolutionary convention of identifying blue-blooded dogs and their owners eternalized in royal portraits, Belcher remains clear and steadfast in his thick metal collar. Offering us a full-face view which, like the head-on portrait photographs that would proliferate in the next decade, the painting records for eternity the maximum material, if not psychological truth, about the sitter. It was the kind of physiognomical document—straightforwardly commemorative, dignified, and identified by name—that, like its human counterparts, would have infinite progeny as the population of pets and pet owners expanded in the nineteenth and twentieth centuries, when the business of painting and photographing beloved dogs would move to the level of international commerce.

As instant signifiers of social identity, dogs loomed large in the work of Realist artists concerned with mirroring the new facts—rich and poor, urban and agrarian—of mid-century life. It was predictable that the most robust and proletarian of the great Realist painters, Gustave Courbet (1819–1877), dedicated as he was to depicting the coarse cross sections of the rural France he knew firsthand, generally included earthy and nondescript mongrels as part of the community rituals of hunting, dining, burying the dead. But even Courbet could learn to ascend the social ladder of canine and human company. So it was that in September 1866, when he had already become an establishment figure in the Paris art world, Courbet was invited to spend a month at the luxurious villa of the Comte de Choiseul. There, pampered and respected, he must have enjoyed the contrast between Second Empire high life on the Normandy coast at Deauville and his own rural origins in the Franche-Comté. And there, too, he recorded a pair of the count's highly bred greyhounds *(fig. 21)*, a far cry from the mongrels, mastiffs, and hunting dogs that belonged to the artist's customary social niche. Yet for all that they may symbolize the pinnacle of French mid-century aristocracy, the count's greyhounds have a surprisingly natural, even awkward air. The setting itself, a trinity of gritty beach, foaming sea, and cloud-filled blue sky, radiates the kind of outdoor freshness that Monet and Boudin (who were also to be guests at the count's villa) were capturing in their contemporary views of the Channel coast; and against this tonic screen of raw, uninhabited nature, the dogs seem momentarily liberated in the sea breeze. Forcing our eye level down, so that we look up at them as we would at the haughtiest of aristocratic sitters, the greyhounds nevertheless take candid poses. Their heads seem to twitch alertly, responding to some natural stimulus, and their postures, compressed into the shallowest of

Courbet's spaces, produce vigorous foreshortenings that can surprise us, as in the greyhound at the right, by a head-on confrontation with hindquarters so rugged and muscular that they undermine the message of the elegantly attenuated, almost Egyptian silhouette of the head and right foreleg. One might almost say that the social collisions evident here reflect the Marxian concepts of class struggle. Indeed, the painting must have looked like a conspicuous intruder, half aristocratic, half nouveau riche, when it was exhibited the following year with the retrospective of 115 works Courbet organized for himself as a one-man attraction in Paris's second great World's Fair of 1867.

More conventional, but no less intense a pinpointing of a sentient animal in nature, was another painting of a country dog by an artist of Courbet's Realist generation, Constant Troyon (1810–1865). Associated with the retreat from the city that characterized the rustic milieu of his colleagues in the Barbizon School, Troyon specialized in the painting of rural animals. From 1854 on, he made annual summer visits to the property of his friend and student, another Salon painter, Léon-Félix Loysel, who kept kennels for hunting dogs in the Touraine. One of these pointers was singled out for Troyon's large painting of 1860 that obliges us to empathize, as it were, with the excitement familiar to these dogs' profession *(fig. 22)*. Troyon virtually locates us in a ditch in the open country, right behind the pointer, who, sniffing the air, suddenly seems to be aware of an animal presence. As an occupational portrait, this pointer is clearly the anonymous descendant of those royal hunting dogs depicted by Desportes *(fig. 1)* and his many seventeenth-century Flemish predecessors, but Troyon lends the venerable theme a vivid

reality by communicating the high tensions of this moment in the life of one lone hunting dog. The pointer, as palpably close to us as Courbet's greyhounds, is given unexpected drama by the sweeping autumnal landscape of menacing storm clouds, whose nervous animation is echoed not only in the luminous light-dark contrasts of the dog's spots, but in the high-keyed emotion conveyed by the taut, springlike coil of his lean body, one paw over the ditch in anticipation. Realist in its empirical grasp of animal and landscape, Troyon's painting still carries with it a Romantic sense of uncommon passion that can energize even the most common events.

Far more prose than poetry defines a named portrait of another hunting dog, Barbaro *(fig. 23)*, by the most renowned woman painter of her century, Rosa Bonheur (1822–1899). A specialist in animal painting like Landseer (whose fame she rivaled even in England, where Queen Victoria became both her friend and patron), she left behind the exotic zoological specimens of an earlier French generation of *animaliers*—tigers, gavials, pythons—in favor of domesticated farm animals who provided the counterpart to the peasants so familiar in contemporary Realist painting. In the undated *Barbaro After the Hunt*, a canvas of major dimensions for its minor subject, a rough-haired, low-bred hunting dog is depicted in a winsomely sullen mood. Chained to the wall by a nail that holds his unbuckled collar, Barbaro seems almost to be explaining his comical plight by reference to the bucket and brush at the left, a still life that tells us that he has just been bathed and scrubbed. The crude inscription above, almost like graffiti on a barn wall, is a far cry from the aristocratic lettering on, say, Delaroche's *Belcher (fig. 20)*, and demotes socially this momentarily un-

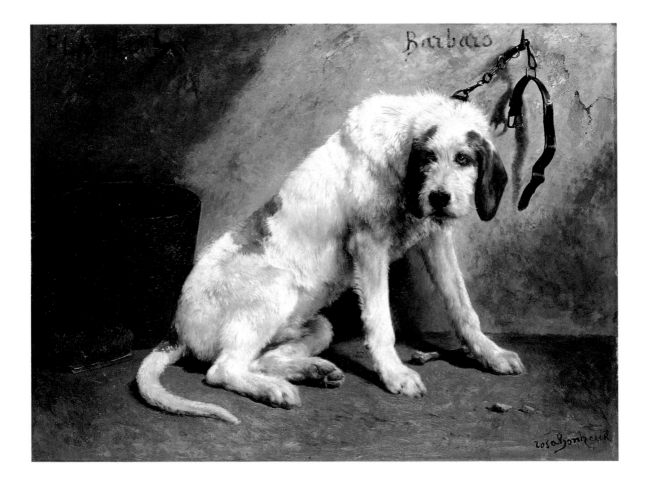

23. Rosa Bonheur

"BARBARO" AFTER THE HUNT

n.d. Oil on canvas, 38 × 51¼″. Philadelphia Museum of Art. Wilstach Collection. Given by John G. Johnson.

happy animal to the level of that unthreatening naïveté which sophisticated painters and patrons in Paris liked to think characteristic of French rural populations. Even the crudely foursquare composition and the earthy tones of brown and gray emphasize this mode of unaffected rustic truth, remote from the fancier structures and palettes used for the upper levels of mid-century social and intellectual hierarchies.

Bonheur's Realist assault on artificial conventions was often mitigated by the trickle of sentiment that would give her dogs or farm animals an extra ration of cuteness or nobility. No such palliatives, however, were applied to what was perhaps the most willfully debunking Realist image of a dog in nineteenth-century art, a diminutive plaster of c. 1880 by the erratic Italian sculptor Adriano Cecioni (1838–1886), which simply documents a dog defecating *(fig. 24)*. Especially by contrast to mid-century conventions of dog sculpture, which ranged from small, exquisitely wrought bronzes of fancy breeds by the French Romantic sculptor Antoine-Louis Barye to lifesize portraits of a beloved Newfoundland like Bashaw *(fig. 16)* or of Prince Albert's favorite greyhound, Eos (modeled by the Prince Consort himself to grace the terrace of his country house, Osborne, on the Isle of Wight), Cecioni's common mutt performing a most common act is a miniature shocker. So low a rung is it on the ladder of subject hierarchies that even within the aesthetic program of what rebellious mid-century Italian artists called Verismo, with its insistence on recording in scrupulous detail the mundane verities of the material world, Cecioni's dog strikes a comically base note.

Proprieties aside, however, this little plaster speaks for the period's relentless insistence on documentation, a search for data that often intersected the goals of scientific investigation. Such goals were clear in the anthologies of analytically dissected visual facts provided by the famous English-born photographer Eadweard Muybridge (1830–1904), who, like many of his European contemporaries, was concerned with precisely controlled records of animals and human beings in motion. Beginning such investigations in 1872 with an enquiry into the positions of racing horse's legs in motion (were all four ever off the ground at the same moment?), Muybridge expanded these laboratory studies to include a wide range of man and beast, finally published in eleven volumes in 1887 under the title *Animal Locomotion*. Dogs figured large in a photographic menagerie that included everything from jumping kangaroos to flying vultures and, like the horses documented, were named in the published plates. A prominent model in this huge photographic compendium is Dread, a mastiff recorded walking, trotting, and galloping in split-second frames that, for the student of comparative anatomy, calibrate in space and time the position of every muscle as the animal moves. In a typical plate of multiple frames *(fig. 25)*, Dread is seen walking in oblique views against a measured graph, a dog who now functions like a living machine in an age that would begin to equate the functioning of the industrial world with that of its inhabitants, both human and animal. It was the kind of quasi-scientific diagrammatic image that was to become deeply rooted in the Western imagination, and by 1912, dogs, as in Balla's Futurist dachshund to appear later in these pages *(fig. 41)*, not to mention people, as in the notorious nude that descends Duchamp's staircase, would conform to this new mechanistic concept of motion that could appear at once objective and fantastic.

If dogs, in the later nineteenth century, could comply with the demands of scientific information, they could also satisfy the highest demands of art, especially when a painter of the stature of Édouard Manet (1832–1883) was involved. Although Manet appears to have been anxious about letting dogs into his studio for fear of damage to his canvases, he nevertheless accepted many commissions for dog portraits. In keeping with the rapid escalation of his subjects from low-class street life in the early 1860s to public and private scenes of greater luxury and refinement, these dog portraits, extending from 1867 to 1882, and including a King Charles spaniel, a Yorkshire terrier, and a Bichon Frise, mirror a pampered lot. Of this anthology, none is so witty, erudite, and exotic as his portrayal of Tama *(fig. 26)*, a Japanese Chin. This breed was first introduced to the West by Commodore Perry in 1853, who received some as a gift from his Japanese hosts, and who in turn offered a pair of these toy dogs to Queen Victoria. Tama's owner, Henri Cernuschi, was an early collector of Far Eastern art, and in the company of Manet's friend, the art critic Théodore Duret, had traveled in the Orient between 1871 and

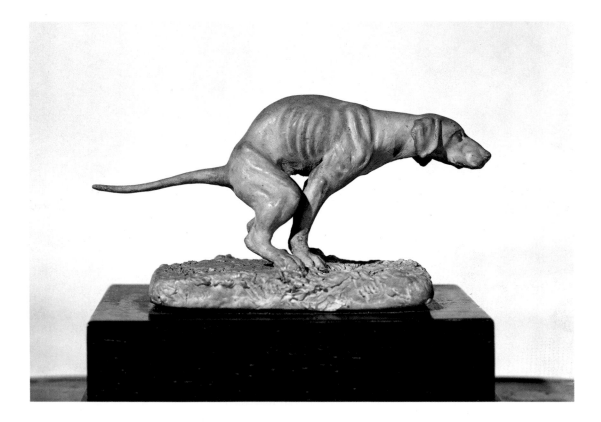

24. Adriano Cecioni

DOG DEFECATING

c. 1880. Plaster, height 3½". Collection Aldo Gonelli, Florence

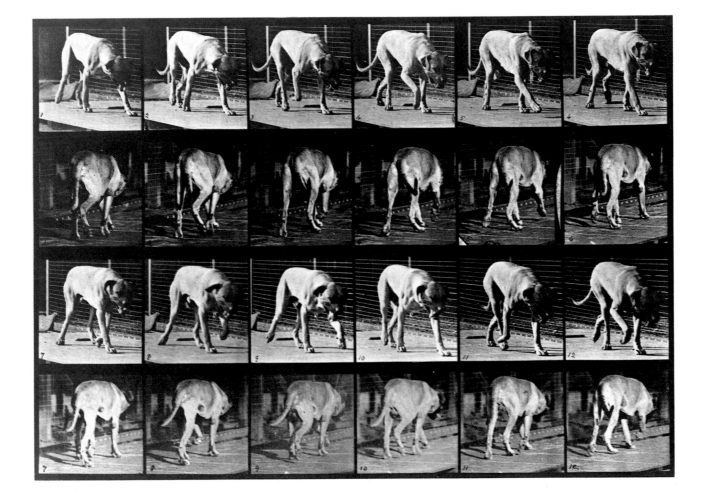

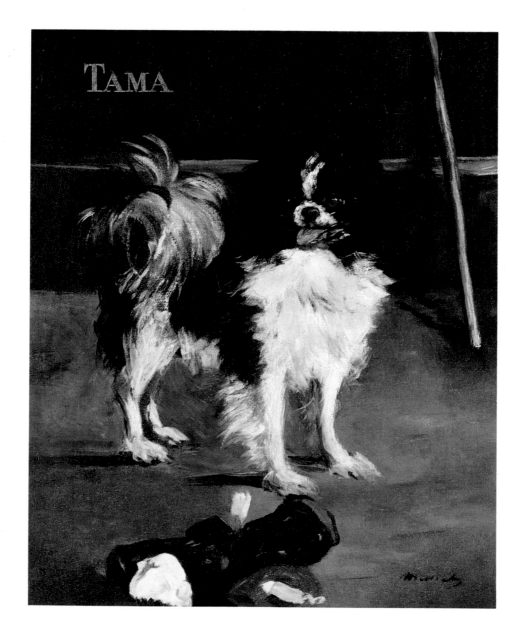

26. Édouard Manet

TAMA, THE JAPANESE DOG

c. 1875. Oil on canvas, 24 × 19½″. From the Collection of Mr. and Mrs. Paul Mellon, Upperville, Virginia

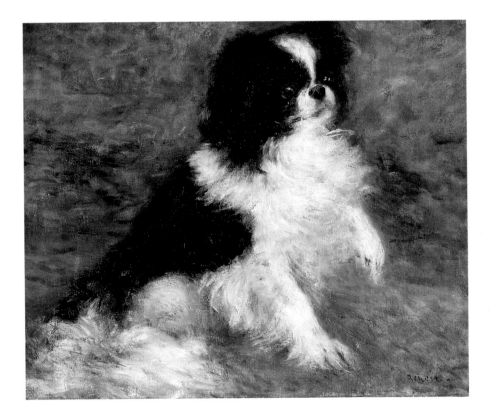

27. *Pierre-Auguste Renoir*

TAMA, THE JAPANESE DOG

c. 1876. Oil on canvas, 15¹¹⁄₁₆ × 18⅛″. Sterling and Francine Clark Art Institute, Williamstown, Massachusetts

1873, accumulating objects that today form the core of the Musée Cernuschi in Paris. Among these precious specimens from an exotic and, to many Western eyes, a magically beautiful culture that could counter the vulgarity of popular mid-century taste, Tama was a living souvenir, whose very name meant "jewel" in Japanese. About 1875, Manet, already immersed in the arts of Japan, painted Tama's portrait, adding, as a reminder of the dog's remote origins, a Japanese doll that lies on the floor with a characteristically studied casualness. Characteristic of Manet, too, is the contracted background, a steep, continuous rise that creates, as in the Japanese prints Manet so enjoyed and absorbed, a flattened plane on top of which silhouetted objects hover in decorative bouquets of paint. But also typical for Manet, art-historical allusions proliferate. If the aesthetic of Japan is appropriately suggested here, so too is that of seventeenth-century Spanish painting, which could similarly prompt Manet to develop a vaguely shallow space upon which to float his delectable brushwork. Most particularly, the court portraiture of Velázquez is evoked, not only by the bravura contrasts of Tama's black-and-white patches and the ennobling inscription above (of a sort that was often added to identify the portrait of an infanta by name), but perhaps by even more specific references to Velázquez's portraits of court dwarfs with dogs, which produce the odd confusion of human and canine scale so conspicuous in the juxtaposition of the diminutive Tama and the still smaller doll. Moreover, Manet's pleasure in conjuring up, as in a parody, other works of art may even include in this unexpected composition a sly look backward to his own work, the now fragmented painting from the 1864 Salon of a victorious bull in a ring, hovering triumphantly over the supine body of a dead bull-fighter.

Happily, the intellectual sparkle of these art-historical associations is matched by the sheer dazzle of the small canvas itself, in which the austere and geometrically lucid background provides a surprising setting for the explosion of feathery paint that makes Tama's fur palpable and for the cool reds in the Japanese artifact that lies at the dog's feet.

By a fortunate coincidence, Tama was also painted not once but twice by another great Impressionist, Pierre-Auguste Renoir (1840–1919), providing what is almost a textbook contrast between the two artists. In the larger of these two small canvases of about 1876 *(fig. 27)*, the crackling elegance and cerebral wit of Manet have dissolved into the archetypal image of cuddly Renoir fluff. Both eyes on a master and one obedient paw in the air, Tama sweetly evaporates into a softly mottled background. Unabashedly adored and adorable, as seen by Renoir, Tama is virtually a resurrection of those miniature poodles so familiar in the French Rococo art that helped to create the artist's own smiling and sensuously comforting style and that cast its hedonistic spell across so many other Impressionist paintings. As such, next to Manet's *Tama*, Renoir's portrait of this bit of canine *japonisme* could hardly define more succinctly the gulf of style and personality that separates these two masters.

Manet's and Renoir's dog portraits were hardly unique in the Impressionist milieu, which also included Berthe Morisot's portrait of Mallarmé's Shakespearean greyhound, Laertes. And now that recent research has begun to explore the lesser lights of the period, we know that at that landmark exhibition, the first Impressionist group show of 1874, not only did artists named Renoir, Degas, Monet, and Cézanne show their work, but also artists whose names are hardly household words. Among these

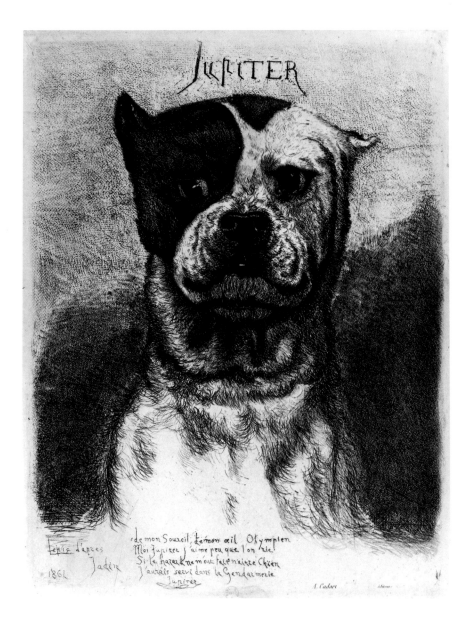

28. Vicomte Lepic

JUPITER (PORTRAIT DE CHIEN)

Impressionist Exhibition, 1874. Etching, after a painting by Louis Jadin. Bibliothèque Nationale, Paris

was a dog breeder, aristocrat, and friend of Degas's, the Vicomte Ludovic-Napoléon Lepic (1839–1899), whose name has survived mainly through Degas's extraordinary portrait of him, his two daughters, and his elegant greyhound caught walking across the Place de la Concorde. But Lepic belongs in the annals of Impressionism not only as a sitter, but as an artist whose repertory included portraits of the fancy dogs he bred, knew, and owned, as well as etchings after other artists' dog portraits. Two of these, in fact, appeared at the first Impressionist exhibition, etchings of a terrier named Caesar and an English bulldog named Jupiter, grandly Roman names that perpetuated, now with a satirical twist, earlier traditions of dog nomenclature in which classical erudition was taken more for granted (as in Neptune for a Newfoundland). In *Jupiter (fig. 28)*, an etching after a painting by Louis Jadin shown at the 1861 Salon, the sitter follows the format (and the breed) of Delaroche's *Belcher* of 1832 *(fig. 20)*, but his strained frontality and grandeur are clearly spoofs on his Olympian identity, a point underscored as parody in the French quatrain written below the print, translatable as: "From my brow and Olympian eye, I, Jupiter, dislike seeing people laugh. If I had not by accident been born a dog, I would have been a member of the police force." Such a joke continues to undermine that faith in classical subject matter still perpetuated by conservative art academies but challenged, at the same time, by exactly such communal displays of modernity as the one in which these dog portraits figured, a diverse anthology quickly to be baptized "Impressionism."

As for this modernity, few dogs could capture as many truths about late nineteenth-century Paris as another bulldog swiftly sketched in 1897 by Henri de Toulouse-Lautrec (1864–1901) as a first idea for a lithograph destined for a menu *(fig. 29)*. The dog, Bouboule (a French nickname that, applied to dogs and people, suggests a pudgy, butterball face and physique), belonged to a certain Mme Palmyre, who ran a well-known lesbian restaurant, La Souris, in that seedy, underground milieu Toulouse-Lautrec embraced in both his life and his art. As is so often noticed about dogs and their owners, Bouboule was said to resemble Mme Palmyre, or vice versa, both of them seemingly gruff and belligerent, but having barks louder than their bites. Nevertheless, Bouboule, unlike his mistress, presumably disliked women, and according to eyewitness accounts, often ducked under the restaurant tables and urinated on the clients' dresses. Even without being privy to such stories, we can tell, thanks to Toulouse-Lautrec's genius at instant characterization, that this dog is a memorably streetwise Parisian, a vivid personality in the portrait gallery of fin-de-siècle entertainers and social outcasts created by the artist in the 1890s. Nervously alert from ears to belly, Bouboule seems to be quivering before our eyes, about to growl or snap at any trespasser. We recognize the truth of what André Rivoire wrote about Toulouse-Lautrec in 1901, just after the artist's death: ". . . as in fables, animals became persons for him. . . . He made portraits of animals as he made portraits of men."

Although he may conjure up an entire social milieu, Bouboule is, like Toulouse-Lautrec's other sitters, unforgettably individual. But the other extreme, the dog as a generalized symbol in society, also made its appearance within the most adventurous territories explored by French artists emerging after the heyday of Impressionism, and nowhere more indelibly than in the masterpiece by Georges

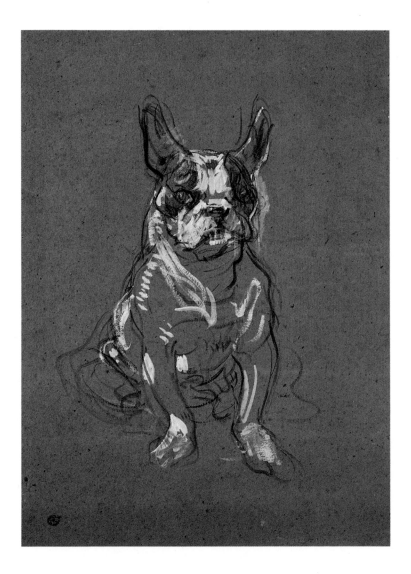

29. Henri de Toulouse-Lautrec

BOUBOULE: MME. PALMYRE'S BULLDOG

1897. Pastel drawing on board. Musée Toulouse-Lautrec, Albi

Seurat (1859–1891) that made its debut at the last Impressionist exhibition of 1886, there titled *A Sunday at the Grande-Jatte (1884)*, the parenthesized date referring to the year in which it was conceived and begun. Painstakingly working out every complex detail of the parts and the whole in 1884–85, Seurat made many studies of the landscape setting on this sliver of an isle in the Seine, sometimes leaving it hauntingly empty, sometimes populating it with the people, dogs, and monkey to be fixed into eternal place in the large finished painting. Among these preliminary rehearsals for that motionless drama, one singles out a lone inhabitant of the Grande-Jatte,

the black mongrel who, center stage, is without mistress or master, sniffing the ground like a stray dog in search of food, shelter, or love *(fig. 30)*. Never lost in the crowd, even in the completed painting, this dog, as seen in the vibrantly granular shadows Seurat created by drawing with greasy conté crayon on thick rag paper, seems charged with a particular poignancy, a lone scavenger on a pleasure island after the visitors have departed. Indeed, the sociological thrust of recent interpretations of the *Grande-Jatte* is borne out here; for the solitary, homeless dog in the painting has been discussed by the art historian Richard Thomson as representing a disruptive new

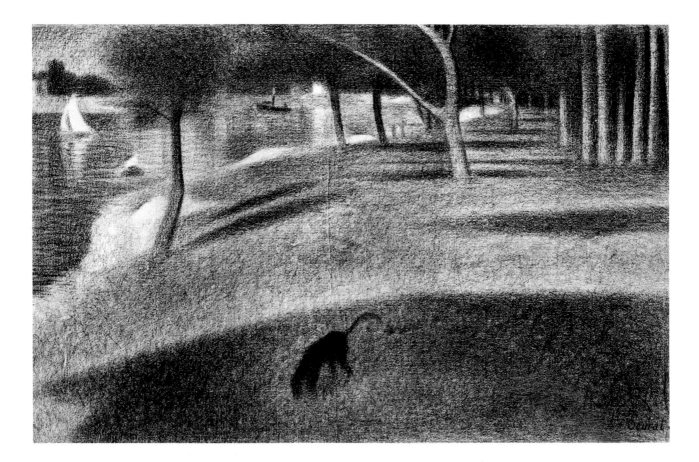

30. Georges Seurat

STUDY FOR LA GRANDE-JATTE: LANDSCAPE WITH DOG

c. 1884-85. Conte crayon, 15¾ × 23⅝″. British Museum, London

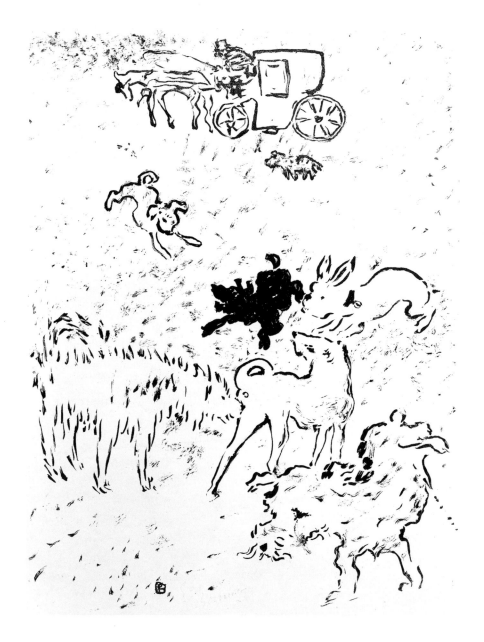

31. Pierre Bonnard

DOGS, ONE OF A SERIES OF FOUR PUBLISHED IN *L'ESCARMOUCHE*
1893. Lithograph, printed in black, 14⁷⁄₁₆ × 10¼″. Collection The Museum of Modern Art, New York.
Gift of Abby Aldrich Rockefeller

kind of social class, wandering pariahs, as yet un-claimed and uncategorized, of a type earlier recognizable in Gustave Caillebotte's views of Parisian thoroughfares. Seen in downcast solitude against a landscape now so familiar to us that the mind's eye can immediately conjure up its other *dramatis personae*, the black mongrel in this drawing corroborates just such a reading, a homeless new city dweller who will remain alone in public places after the better-heeled crowds come and go, as he does so pointedly here.

Parisian street dogs, however, could also suggest a more cheerful community spirit, especially in the harmonious vision of Pierre Bonnard (1867–1947), who, in the 1890s, created the supplest variations on the theme of a sweetly untroubled, middle-class Paris. In both his indoor and outdoor vignettes, we can almost savor Proustian memories of the quiet, comforting rhythms of French domesticity at its most refined, whether in the nursery, the dining room, or the market street. Domesticated animals figure throughout, gently cushioning interiors as they do even an open street in a lithograph of 1893 simply titled *Dogs (fig. 31)*. Sensitive to the most flickering nuances of patterned, almost textiled surfaces in the medium of paint, watercolor, or print, Bonnard nearly camouflages here this frisky canine society in a flurry of graphic shorthand, from long and short dots to miniature wriggles. But these bodiless touches of the lithographic crayon, floating, it would seem, like snowflakes, can also become quite specifically legible, soon defining an encounter of six completely different breeds on a Paris street that frolic together with almost catlike agility as, in the distance, a tiny dog passes by in tandem with a horse-drawn carriage. In Bonnard's view, so different

from Seurat's, the streets of Paris offer an enchanting playground for dogs. Indeed, two years before, in 1891, Bonnard had executed a watercolor design for a large cabinet (never, alas, built) that would have been covered with gamboling, somersaulting dogs, a fairy-tale environment of total joie de vivre.

Only a decade later, in 1901, the amazing child prodigy of photography, Jacques-Henri Lartigue (1894–1986), was given a hand camera at the age of seven, and immediately began to record the same seductions of *belle époque* Paris that Bonnard had so lovingly mirrored in the 1890s. In Lartigue's affluent world, everything seems to be in buoyant, cheerful motion, from homemade flying machines and new-fangled automobiles to spurting fountains and skirts swept by sea winds at elegant resorts. And his thoroughbred dogs, of course—Afghan hounds or Jack Russells—are no less happy and volatile, conveying a childlike optimism of spirit that lasted, anachronistically, far beyond the nightmare of the First World War. So it is that in a photo of Lartigue's own pet, Toby, taken in 1923 *(fig. 32)*, we feel that one of Bonnard's frisky and carefree dogs has somehow survived as a reminder of what some might have experienced as the endlessly pleasurable life of Paris 1900, a nostalgic fiction we may still cling to today. As Lartigue himself was to put it in his comment on the photograph: "Look at my dog Toby: doesn't he seem to have endless possibilities before him?"

Lartigue's infectiously heartening spirit, justified by his own good fortune, was completely personal. His was a far cry from the public myths of optimism about the human race propagated in later nineteenth-century art, where anonymous dogs, like anonymous children, continued to provide touching or

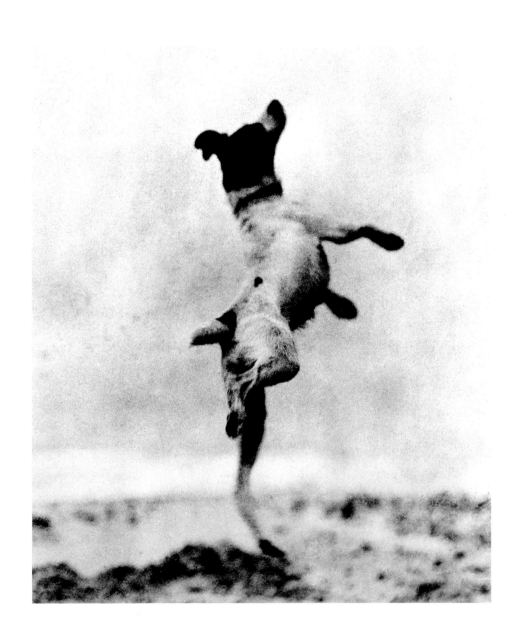

32. Jacques-Henri Lartigue

TOBY

1923. Photograph. Copyright Association des Amis de J. H. Lartigue

ennobling examples of old-fashioned virtuous be-havior, as well as dependable triggers to set off, in vastly growing popular audiences, smiling re-sponses to naive cuteness and charm. The domain of what in a more cynical, post-Victorian world is con-veniently classified as kitsch includes a global popu-lation of dogs who reflect, in a roseate vision of Garden-of-Eden simplicity and innocence, the best of human nature. Take, for example, *The Happy Mother* by the Scottish painter Robert Alexander (1840–1923), shown first in Edinburgh in 1887 at the Royal Scottish Academy's annual exhibition *(fig. 33)*. Like many of these proliferating Victorian icons of natural goodness, this one has eighteenth-century roots, for it seems the direct descendant of Oudry's rustic canine maternity of 1752 *(fig. 2)*. Here, a sable-and-white collie—the local Scottish working-class breed and a progenitor of that famous Hollywood starlet of the 1940s, Lassie—proudly displays her eight newborn puppies who reside in humble happiness inside a barnyard enclosure furnished with straw and a makeshift box kennel. Unlike Oudry's scene of rural motherhood, Alex-ander's looks too good to be true, particularly when considered as another specimen of the nineteenth century's endless pictorial whitewashing of the harshest urban and agrarian realities under images of plain, heartfelt felicity. Unlike the cold, aban-doned, and starving children born to Britain's ex-panding city and country populations, these collie puppies are warmed, loved, and fed by an ideal mother, while the father, to be sure, is happily em-ployed outdoors by a shepherd. Similarly, the low-liest of occupations—for instance, the extermina-tion of vermin by small and adorable terriers, skilled at ratting—was a common subject among Victorian

dog painters, offering, as it were, a charming canine equivalent to the brutal realities of the unspeakable lives led by armies of child laborers in farms and factories, who might be ratters themselves, or work at anything from chimney sweep to unskilled miner.

The uncommon fidelity, as well as Christian pi-ety, traditionally associated with dogs in their em-blematic role in tomb sculpture and sacramental oaths could also be transformed by the late nine-teenth century into images that almost caricature ex-tremes of devotion, often exceeding even Landseer's most popular narratives of dogs who mourn their masters with a grief and steadfastness rare in the hu-man species. Such is the case in *Requiescat*, submit-ted to the Royal Academy exhibition of 1888 by a specialist in animal and genre painting, Briton Ri-vière (1840–1920). Although Rivière's repertory of subject matter encompassed dogs in contemporary genre situations of city and country low-life, he also explored a sweeping and conventionally lofty range of literary and historical sources, from Homer to the Bible, in order to find narrative passages (such as the disposition of Hector's body or the story of Lazarus) that featured dogs. This erudite mobility could even include the Middle Ages. In *Requiescat*, a dog's prayer for the dead that was repeated in a smaller version of 1889 *(fig. 34)*, the canine mourner, fa-miliar in Landseer, has been transported to a Gothic world of knights and armor. Here, a traditional late medieval tomb sculpture (recalling particularly the gilded copper effigy of Edward the Black Prince in Canterbury Cathedral) with a dog as an emblem of Fidelity is recreated in what resembles a Victorian High Gothic charade similar to the cenotaph of Prince Albert at Windsor. Stretched out with ar-chaic stiffness on a richly embroidered drapery that

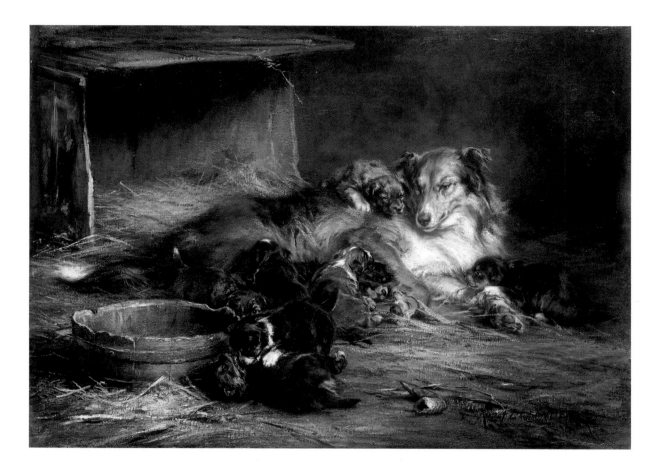

33. Robert Alexander

THE HAPPY MOTHER

1887. Oil on canvas, 31¼ × 45″. National Gallery of Scotland, Edinburgh

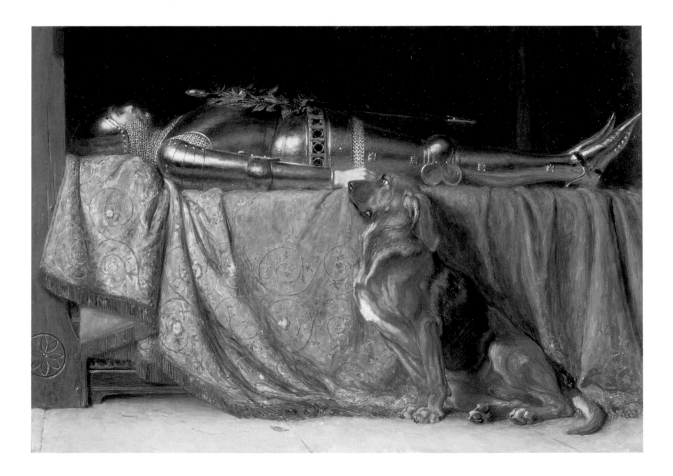

34. Briton Rivière

REQUIESCAT

1889. Oil on canvas, 25 × 53¾". The Forbes Magazine Collection, New York

looks like the product of the British Arts and Crafts Movement of the 1880s, the dead knight is attended, after the human mourners have left, by his loyal and large bloodhound, who sits by his wooden deathbed, eyes tearing, jowls drooping, in a profile posture nearly as rigid, in its neo-medieval planarity, as that of its master. If only, the message reads, human beings, in this or any other age, could be counted on for such selfless and prayerful devotion!

The same theme, translated this time to the technological world of the later nineteenth century, is found in what is surely the best known of all dog pictures and arguably the most frequently reproduced painting in the world, '*His Master's Voice*' (*fig. 35*), by the otherwise forgotten artist Francis Barraud (1856–1924). A painter of sentimental Victorian narratives, Barraud had begun in 1881 to exhibit at the Royal Academy, which, however, rejected '*His Master's Voice*' in 1899 when the work was completed. But this official slur was more than compensated for by the painting's subsequent fame, which is so great and so global that, as in the case of its rival for instant recognition anywhere on this planet, the Mona Lisa, tales have been spun around it, including one that claims the painting originally showed the coffin of the artist's brother, as well as the phonograph playing the voice of the deceased, a feature that would bring it closer to the funereal mood of Rivière's *Requiescat*. But more likely, at least according to the artist's own later account, the painting was simply inspired by the puzzled but intelligent reaction of his pet terrier Nipper (whom he cared for after his brother's death) to the sound of a voice played back on the phonograph, prompting this painted tribute to a dog's ability to respond discerningly and loyally to, in the words of the title, '*His Master's Voice*.' In a way that typified the fre-

quent adaptation of ostensibly respectable academic paintings to the flourishing advertising business in the later nineteenth century (the use of John Everett Millais's painting of 1886, *Bubbles*, for the Pears Soap ad is the best-known example), Barraud had in mind selling his image. He copyrighted it on 11 February 1899, and quickly offered it to the Edison Bell Company, which turned it down. But The Gramophone Company bought it that September, requesting that Barraud change the "talking machine" of the original painting, the Edison phonograph with its cylinder disk, to its own newer product, a gramophone with a flat disk first patented in 1897, in time to appear in the company's advertising literature in January 1900. Thereafter, Nipper's image would spend the rest of the twentieth century crossing the Atlantic and every other ocean, becoming one of the world's most famous logos, a dog so beloved that in 1984, on what was calculated to be the centenary of his birth, a group of business executives and entertainers gathered to commemorate with two plaques the dog's grave in a car park behind a London branch of Lloyds Bank. Unwittingly, one feels that Barraud, in '*His Master's Voice*,' invented a brilliantly seamless continuity between the most venerable traditions of canine fidelity and a brand new world of twentieth-century technology and publicity. In the words of The Gramophone Company's own advertising copy of the 1950s, "The strong appeal of the picture lies probably in the fidelity of the dog. It is appropriate therefore that this quality of fidelity has been the keynote of '*His Master's Voice*' ever since—fidelity in the reproduction of the works of great musical artists—fidelity to the public who have relied upon '*His Master's Voice*' for half a century to provide the latest and best in home entertainment."

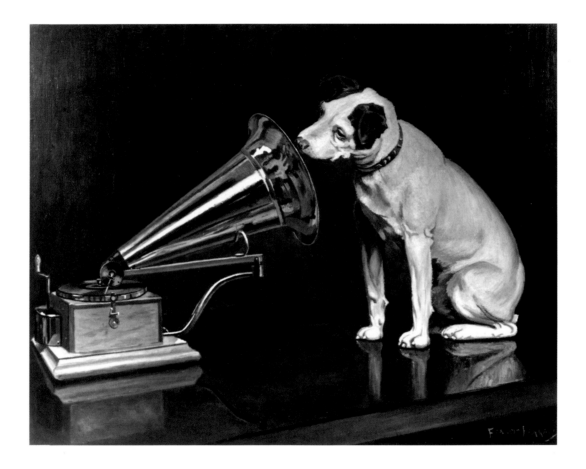

35. Francis Barraud

'HIS MASTER'S VOICE'

c. 1898–99. Oil on canvas, 36 × 28″. Courtesy of BMG Music/RCA Records

Irresistible canine poses and the demands of modern commerce also account for a painting as arresting, if hardly as renowned as Barraud's, an *Optician's Sign* of 1902 by the illustrious French academician Jean-Léon Gérôme (1824–1904), whose magically hyper-realist paintings are now in the forefront of revisionist revaluation. Occupying a position of conservative authority in the second half of the nineteenth century comparable to that of Ingres in the first half, Gérôme, like Ingres before him, painted many dogs, using them as scrupulously accurate props in his glassy reconstructions that ranged from Greco-Roman antiquity (Diogenes living in a barrel alongside the street dogs of Athens) to contemporary North Africa (elegant Arab hunting dogs), an exotic milieu that would make his international fame. Moreover, Gérôme's fondness for dogs was reflected in a series of relatively conventional dog portraits of sitters named *Laddie*, *Boy*, and *Said*. But at the end of his life, in 1902, Gérôme contributed to an exhibition sponsored by the City of Paris of advertising signs made by established artists. For this he made an optician's sign, creating a dog at once so real and so fantastic that it almost belongs to the twentieth century in spirit as it literally does in date *(fig. 36)*. The cutest of terriers, sitting up to stop the hardest-hearted customers in their tracks, is depicted with the photographic precision familiar to Gérôme's sharp-focus technique, but this illusion is immediately canceled by the flat, fragmented inscription below—O PTI CIEN—a pun that simultaneously reads in French as *opticien*, and as *O, petit chien*, or *Au petit chien* ("Oh, little dog," or "At the [sign of the] little dog"). To confound this image further, the terrier's mock-dignified monocle is topped by a huge floating pince-nez, behind which a pair of human eyes eerily stare us down. And as an extra joke, Gérôme,

as an off-duty academician, has signed his name on the flat ground with a mock-classic seriousness, offering the printed inscription in a mix of French and Latin: J. L. GEROME BARBOUILLAVIT ANNO DOMINI 1902, that is, "Daubed by J. L. Gérôme...." As for the frame, these whimiscal, yet disquieting undercurrents expand to three fantastic dimensions that, like the painting, shuffle fact and fiction, large and small. Above center, a cyclopean eye appears to be magnified in a magic glass; at upper left and right, tiny binoculars invite distant inspection; and below, a miniature pince-nez with tinted blue lenses suggests that the spectator scrutinize the canvas with myopic closeness.

If the sentiment here belongs to the domain of Nipper in the Land of Modern Inventions, the bizarre juxtapositions unexpectedly herald aspects of Dada and Surrealism, a point first made in 1967 by none other than Salvador Dalí, who saw in Gérôme's advertising sign not only a preview of Duchamp's notorious moustached Mona Lisa (with its inscribed pun, *LHOOQ*, meaning *look* as well as the French obscenity *Elle a chaud au cul*), but quite obviously of Dalí's own brand of Surrealism, a "dream photograph" whose uncommonly intense reality, especially when coupled with the disembodied eyes so familiar to Surrealist iconography, could unbalance completely our grasp of the mundane, material world.

It is only by an ironic accident that, with one atypical painting, Gérôme, the academic realist and sworn opponent to all innovation in late nineteenth-century painting, might appear a precursor of the most irrational currents of our own century. There is no doubt, however, about the willfully unacademic character of one of the most surprising dog pictures of the late nineteenth century, the *Still Life*

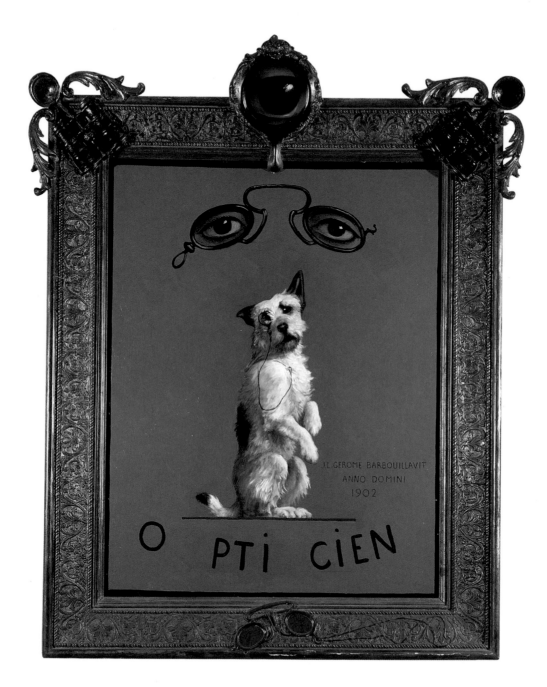

36. Jean-Léon Gérôme

OPTICIAN'S SIGN (O PTI CIEN)

1902. Oil on canvas, 33 × 26″. Private collection

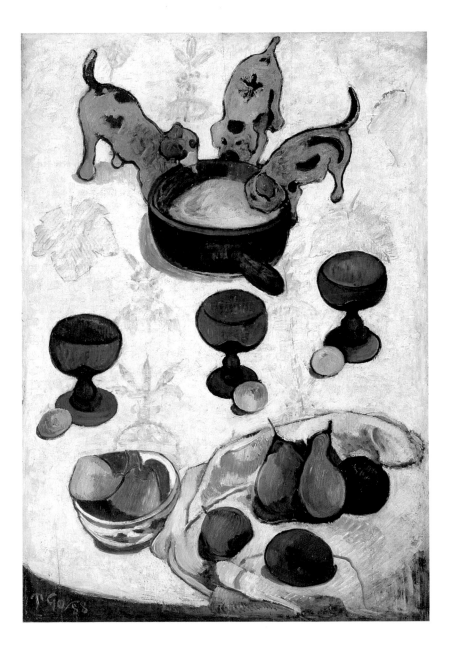

37. Paul Gauguin

STILL LIFE WITH THREE PUPPIES

1888. Oil on wood, 36⅛ × 24⅝″. Collection The Museum of Modern Art, New York. Mrs. Simon Guggenheim Fund

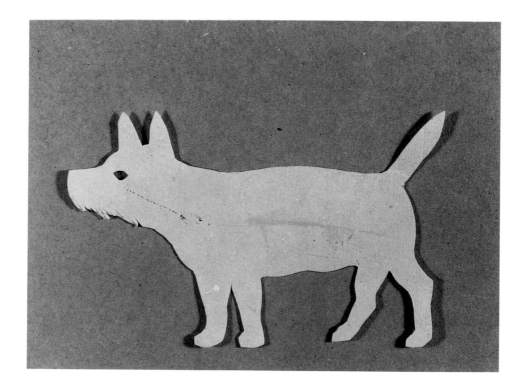

38. Pablo Picasso

D O G

c. 1893–94. Cut-out paper, 2⅛ × 3⅝″. Museo Picasso, Barcelona

with Three Puppies painted by Paul Gauguin (1848–1903) in 1888, the watershed year of his artistic and personal life *(fig. 37)*. A reflection of the miraculous transformation of his art in Brittany, at Pont-Aven, where during nine months, from February to October, he turned the realist premises of Impressionism inside out and upside down, this unprecedented dog painting creates the aura of a fairy tale, childlike in feeling and in style. Gauguin, in fact, had been attracted to a wide anthology of counter-realist styles—Japanese prints, folk art, medieval stained glass—that could help him flee from a world of mere perception into a domain of primitive imagination, and among these catalysts were children's book illustrations by the British artists Randolph Caldecott and Kate Greenaway.

In *Still Life with Three Puppies*, we sense the elementary nursery rhythms of ritual and mystery, in this case the ABC magic of three, as in The Three Little Pigs, Goldilocks and the Three Bears, The Love for Three Oranges, or, as has been suggested, what Gauguin may have conceived in 1888 as a new Holy Artistic Trinity of himself and his equally rebellious artist friends, Denis and Van Gogh. Against the counter-illusionistic audacity of a ground plane so steeply tilted upward that every object floats as if conjured up by a magician's wand, a potentially sentimental vignette of three puppies lapping milk from a crude peasant bowl initiates an excursion to an unnamed mythical realm. The dogs themselves, especially the center puppy with its somewhat sinister slanting eyes and its symmetrical markings which match the decorative floral pattern muffled under the white background, evoke some remote legend, an intuition supported below by the three blue goblets, accompanied by three flattened Cézannesque apples, objects that might be found on the

table of a coarsely painted Last Supper or in some distant realm described in Breton folklore. Indeed, one wonders whether the puppies, combined with the intentionally simple style of clear contour drawing and intensely opaque color, might find their source not only, as has been suggested in a Japanese print, but in one of the British children's-book illustrations Gauguin so admired. Typically for Gauguin's new Symbolist mode, all is evocation, eluding particular narrative description. Typically, too, the sweet little puppies in this wide-eyed fantasy of childhood innocence and mystery only mirror part of the artist's complex personality, since another, more earthily adult part is disclosed by his monogram signature, P GO, a phonetic pun on his name as well as on the word *pego*, which in the French maritime slang of the period means penis. (These three puppies, in fact, were not the only dogs Gauguin joined to the sexual alter ego of his monogram; for at the end of his life, in 1901, when he was living in total debauchery in the Marquesas, he named his housedog Pego.) Flouting every convention of propriety, realism, and narrative in order to discover a world of his own visual and imaginative construction, Gauguin, in this strange still life, could hardly have announced more clearly twentieth-century things to come, whether the worship of a would-be primitive simplicity of form and feeling or the almost religious respect for a space so flat that it virtually coincides with the actual surface of the canvas.

Such a description might also accommodate an even more precocious work of the next decade, a dog's paper silhouette cut out in La Coruña in 1893–94 by an artist named Pablo Ruiz Picasso (1881–1973), who was then barely a teen-ager *(fig. 38)*. Like Runge's paper cutout of c. 1800 *(fig. 17)*, Picasso's follows a long and popular tradition of

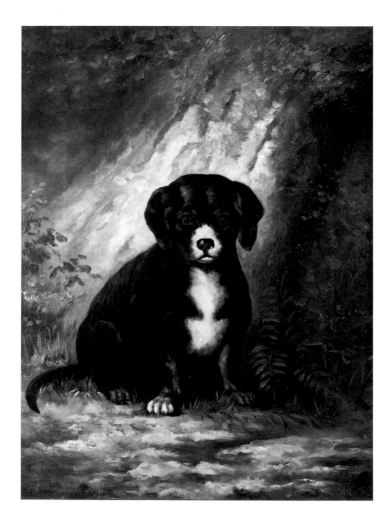

39. Piet Mondrian

PUPPY

1891. Oil on canvas, 20½ × 15¾″. Private collection

silhouette-making, and one particularly enjoyed by children creating their first profile images. In Picasso's case, this cutout might be considered just another document from his prodigious juvenilia, remarkable for its sharp-eyed and skillful intrusion of such realist details as the shaggy fur under the neck that transforms this flat ideogram almost into a specific portrait, probably of Klipper, the pet dog Picasso had at the time (and would paint a year later). But in Picasso, everything connects, and now this throwaway cutout, with its cutout dove as a pendant, reverberates ahead to the innovative years of collage Cubism, when, beginning in 1912, the master would again make paste-and-paper silhouettes to symbolize, as in a child's lexicon, the most familiar objects, depriving them of weight and substance, but miraculously maintaining their sense of a particular reality. And even more specifically, this tiny cutout foreshadows the black painted silhouette of a dog almost camouflaged beneath the table in one of the two versions of *The Three Musicians* of 1921 (Museum of Modern Art, New York). Dogs, like everything in the visible world, turn up often in Picasso's art. But as in his life, which seemed never to be lived without a pet dog, they are almost always depicted with human companions (or at times, even confounded grotesquely with a human head, as in the case of the monstrous portraits of Dora Maar whose face seems to have taken on the physiognomy of Kasbec, the pet Afghan hound of the late 1930s). A dog alone is seldom encountered in Picasso's work, and as such, this juvenile cutting is rare not only in subject, but important as a surprising preview of the techniques and flattened ideograms that, from 1912 on, would revolutionize the art of Picasso and that of his century.

A far more subliminal preview of radically new developments in early twentieth-century art can be found in one last puppy of the 1890s, a canvas of 1891 by, of all unlikely artists, the pioneer of pure geometric abstraction, Piet Mondrian (1872–1944). Painted when he was only nineteen, a year before he matriculated at the Amsterdam Academy, Mondrian's *Puppy (fig. 39)* at first seems only a juvenile exercise in the territory of nineteenth-century sentimental art, a little puppy, far more innocent than Gauguin's, seen in a gentle landscape. But closer observation, fortified by the hindsight of our awareness of Mondrian's mystical development from matter to spirit, reveals an uncommonly intense stare in this puppy, who, with iconic frontality, seeks and fixes the spectator's gaze. Unexpectedly transforming a nineteenth-century formula for producing an indulgent smile into a penetrating eye-to-eye confrontation, this little dog announces the theme of eyes as windows of the soul that would become so conspicuous in Mondrian's portraits of himself and of wide-eyed children in 1901. It was a path from the outer, material world to inner territories of bodiless feeling and spirit that would soon attract not only Mondrian, but such other pioneers of abstract art as Kandinsky, and one that, as recent research has emphasized, would find an official, quasi-religious program in the occult doctrines of Mme Blavatsky and Theosophy, which Mondrian soon espoused. Odd as Mondrian's little puppy in a landscape might seem as a tentative vehicle for a teen-age artist to peek into otherworldly domains, it was an idea that, within two decades, could be amplified to disarmingly metaphysical dimensions, as our first truly twentieth-century dog, Franz Marc's of 1912, may now demonstrate.

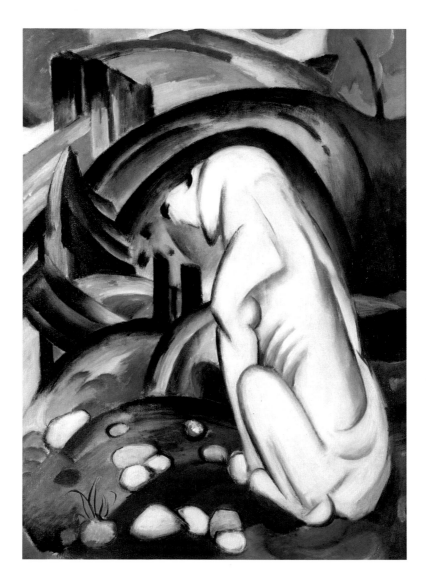

40. Franz Marc

DOG BEFORE THE WORLD (HUND VOR DER WELT)

1912. Oil on canvas, 43¾ × 32¾″. Private collection, Switzerland

· I I I ·

FROM MODERNISM TO

POST·MODERNISM

But suddenly down the wind came tearing a smell sharper,
stronger, more lacerating than any—a smell that ripped across
his brain stirring a thousand instincts, releasing a million
memories—the smell of hair, the smell of fox. Off he flashed
like a fish drawn in a rush through water further and further.
He forgot his mistress; he forgot all humankind.

Virginia Woolf, F L U S H *(London, 1933)*

If asked to pick the year that pinpointed the fever pitch of innovation and international ferment in the chronicle of early twentieth-century art, most art historians would vote for 1912. So it is perhaps no accident that in this year, a German and an Italian artist painted dogs who polarize, in culturally schematic terms, the crisis of the Western world on the brink of the Great War.

The first example is from the hand of the German Franz Marc (1880–1916), a painting that reaches the ultimate extreme of empathy between man, beast, and landscape in a world that has never known human greed and folly *(fig. 40)*. Its usual German title, *Hund vor der Welt*, loses much of its cosmic resonance when translated as *Dog Before the World*. However, the painting itself does convey the uncanny sense that a large white dog, like a meditative philosopher or poet, is seated on its haunches actively contemplating a primordial setting that almost radiates from the animal. Marc, it should quickly be said, was primarily an animal painter, but the French classification of *animalier*, with its implications of narrow specialization, would have falsified the grandiosely spiritual ambitions which directed Marc to this subhuman world. Following in the path of many eighteenth-century thinkers and artists who felt that primitive, remote societies represented a truer, better state of human existence, closer to nature and uncorrupted by urban evil, Marc pursued this reasoning still further, finding in animal life the core of pure and honest being. Nature should not be seen as human beings see it, but as animals do. In his own words, "How does a horse see the world, or an eagle, or a doe, or a dog? How wretched and soulless is our convention of placing animals in a landscape that belongs to our eyes, instead of immersing ourselves in the soul of the animal in order to imagine how he sees!" This immersion into a dog's very being is what Marc had in mind here. (He first called the painting "This is how my dog sees the world.") It was an oddly empathic point of view shared by Marc's contemporary, the German poet Rilke, who could write in a love letter, "Can you imagine with me how glorious it is, for example, to see into a dog, in passing—*into* him . . . to ease oneself into the dog exactly at his center, the place out of which he exists as a dog . . . ?" And it was a point of view amplified and explored with exquisite deftness and complexity by Virginia Woolf, whose biography *Flush* (1933) recounts the courtship of Elizabeth Barrett and Robert Browning through the eyes of the pet cocker spaniel who witnessed it. For Marc, however, it was hardly an experimental tour de force, but rather the fullest possible rejection of the grossly material world of human commerce, science, cities, and of the spiritual poverty that he sensed around him, as did his like-thinking associates who helped him to found the Blue Rider group in Munich in 1911–12. From that city, it was easy to escape into the majestic, unpolluted remoteness of the hills and mountains of the Bavarian Alps, and it is just such a timeless, indeed,

arcadian setting (in actuality, the tiny village of Sindelsdorf) that Marc's large white dog confronts. Painted in molten rainbow colors, inspired in turn by the latest chromatic liberations from Paris, the landscape becomes a spiritual Oz that would carry us from the material suggestion of rocks in the foreground to some luminous, dreamlike environment. As for the dog's static, contemplative posture (the front and head turned obliquely away from us so that we may more easily project ourselves into this sentient creature), this belongs to a long German Romantic tradition of representing people, but not yet dogs, facing the infinite mysteries and longings evoked by landscape, whether it be depictions of the exiled Iphigenia, in paintings by Feuerbach, or of anonymous nature worshipers, in paintings by Friedrich. And as for its color, given Marc's concern with the symbolism of the different hues, the dog's whiteness probably connotes a proto-Christian purity of spirit. Although this obsessive regression from human to animal experience may seem a ludicrous private fantasy to most hard-headed spectators today, Marc's wish to annihilate the ugly reality he knew from prewar Germany was hardly singular. With grim irony, his quest for purification through a total destruction of the corrupt, materialist world he was born in was shared by many other artists and poets in Germany. It was a goal to be realized all too soon and all too literally, taking Marc's own life with it on the front at Verdun, halfway through the war.

The other side of this prewar coin is to be found south of the Alps in the Italy of 1912, when the raucous and belligerent Futurist movement reached its peak. In contradistinction to Marc and his German colleagues, these Italians enthusiastically embraced everything that was specifically manmade, industrial, and technological, especially if it concerned the breathtaking new velocities reached in early twentieth-century transportation. For them, the word spirit, as used by Marc, belonged to the remote era of religion and superstition. If Marc preferred horses free in nature, before the dawn of mankind, the Futurists preferred the horsepower of machines. Within their clashing, metallic environment of speeding automobiles, radiant electric lights, and faceless armies of pedestrians and laborers in vector formation, there is one unexpected and unforgettable image of a dog who seems to be on holiday from the exhilarating mechanical jungle of Milan, the center of Futurist animation. It is, of course, the little dachshund painted by the least heavy-handed of the Futurists, Giacomo Balla (1871–1958), while visiting the picturesque and very unindustrial Tuscan hill-town of Montepulciano in May 1912 *(fig. 41)*. There Balla saw his aristocratic pupil, the Contessa Nerazzini, walking her dachshund and transformed the pair into a delightfully witty painting whose angle of vision is as surprising as its juggled contradictions of old and new. We seem to see the world here from a dog's-eye view, and a very low dog's eye, at that. Within its range of vision is the flat, almost abstract plane of the ground, suggesting a smooth white promenade, and only the lower profile of the skirt and shoes worn by its mistress, whose body, from the knees up, looms way above the picture frame. The elegant silhouettes of the collared dog and the fragment of modish female attire suggest the world of chic illustration and fashion plates (the blur of motion even conjuring up the black gauze of a stylish veil), a glimpse of fancy society in the promenade of late nineteenth-century urban life.

But at the same time, this old world of refined manners, rituals, and clothing is charged with a coolly scientific program, didactic as well as diagrammatic in character.

A recent convert to the Futurist faith, Balla offers here one of his earliest attempts to convey, with analytic precision, the illusion of regularized forward motion. Indeed, the original title was *Leash in Motion*, eliminating, as it were, the potentially sentimental intrusion of dog and owner in favor of scientific enquiry. Inspired by the kind of experiment in chronophotography explored first by Muybridge in America *(fig. 25)* and Marey in France, and then by his friend, the Futurist photographer Anton Giulio Bragaglia (who in 1913 was to photograph Balla as a moving blur standing beside this very painting), Balla virtually demonstrated here his colleague Boccioni's provocative contention that a running horse doesn't have four legs, but twenty. And of course, a dachshund, having such short legs and so long a body, might seem, as schematized by Balla, to have considerably more even than that, just as its wagging tail appears in eight places. This puffing little rhythm, like that of one of the low-lying automobiles Balla liked to drive and to paint, is then calibrated against a regular motion of a far slower tempo, the double rotation of the chain-metal leash, and then, once more, against the more rapid to and fro of the left and right of human feet. The repeat pattern of dashes on the actual picture frame and the suggestion of sleekly moving parallel lines across the ground plane add to this look of scientific measurement and documentation, as does the schematic palette of black and white, suggesting not only an abstract diagram but photography. (When the painting made its debut in early 1913 in a Futur-

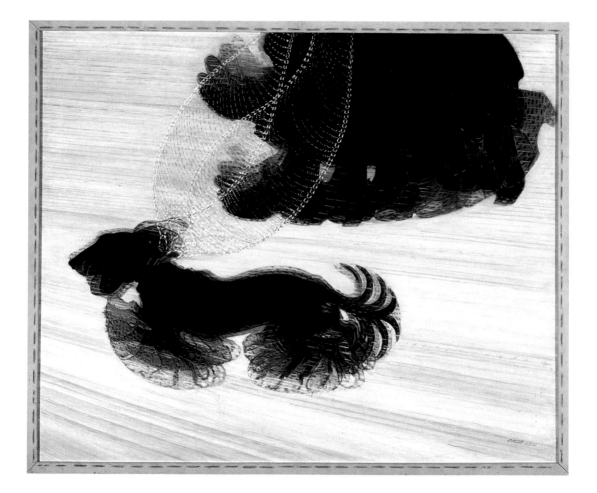

41. *Giacomo Balla*

LEASH IN MOTION

1912. Oil on canvas, 35⅜ × 43¼". Albright-Knox Art Gallery, Buffalo.

Bequest of A. Conger Goodyear and Gift of George F. Goodyear, 1964

ist show in Rome, a critic, Emilio Cecchi, called it "the film of a dachshund that toddles.") Although handled with the lightest tongue-in-cheek touch, which surely recommended it to Duchamp (who later recalled the dent it made on him), Balla's off-duty Futurist painting nevertheless espouses his own and his compatriots' callow enthusiasm for the mechanization they hoped would wrench Italy from its sleepy past and, in 1915, right into the First World War on the side of the Allies. In opposite ways, both Marc's otherworldly white hound and Balla's aristocratic little dachshund reflect the tensions of Europe on the edge of our century's first apocalypse.

No more grim contrast to Marc's faith in spirit and Balla's faith in science could be had than a shattering painting of another dachshund, this time in 1920, on defeated German soil in Dresden. With the rise of bloodthirsty nationalism during the war, the dachshund could become for the Allies not a symbol of chic but of the enemy, the archetypal German dog (for Anglophones in name as well as in origin), and there were even wartime reports in Britain of this breed being stoned by patriots. In Germany, however, it resurfaced as a middle-class urban survivor of the war in a brutal canvas by Otto Dix (1891–1969), who knew the facts of war from his firsthand experience in the German army, which took him to combat in France and Russia. Thereafter Dix devoted the better part of his passionate outrage to exposing, in grisly detail, the realities of the war both on the front and in the human detritus that survived and was sent home. In the *Match Seller* *(fig. 42)*, completed two years after Germany's devastating defeat, Dix gives us another dachshund's-eye view of a public promenade, probably the Pragerstrasse in Dresden. Here, as in Balla's view,

faceless human beings are far above eye level, disappearing in this case, both left and right, in the form of only the lower halves, from tight waists to polished shoes and spats, of well-dressed pedestrians who rush past the grotesque scene in the foreground. As for that, we see on the sidewalk a specimen of the no longer regimented German armies back from the war, this one a quadruple amputee propped before the crowd as a vendor of matches. With painful irony, this piece of military wreckage plays an inert, secondary role in the urban scene, the more active protagonist being someone's pet dachshund, who pauses to piss on the helpless beggar as if he were a tree stump or a fire hydrant. And with still more painful irony, the beggar would have a dog's-eye view of the city, were he not also blind. The hideous clash between the war's human flotsam and jetsam and the reconstructive mood of middle-class business as usual is made still more acute by the shrill contrast between the tidy, geometric patterns of the sidewalk and building facade, immaculately clean, and the soiling of this order, whether with the trickle of urine that runs from the dachshund's lifted leg into the gutter or with the graffiti scribbled in Gothic script that names the wares being shouted from the beggar's mouth ("genuine Swedish matches") and, on the curb, the artist's name and date. In Germany after the war, Dix saw all human and rational hierarchies toppled to the ground, leaving a cityscape where a dachshund can piss on what was once a man.

The retreat from recording the harshest realities of the twentieth century could be as rapid after as before the war; and within the context of German art, the mystical goals of the short-lived Franz Marc could be approached by his close friend and associate in the Blue Rider, the Swiss-born Paul Klee (1879–

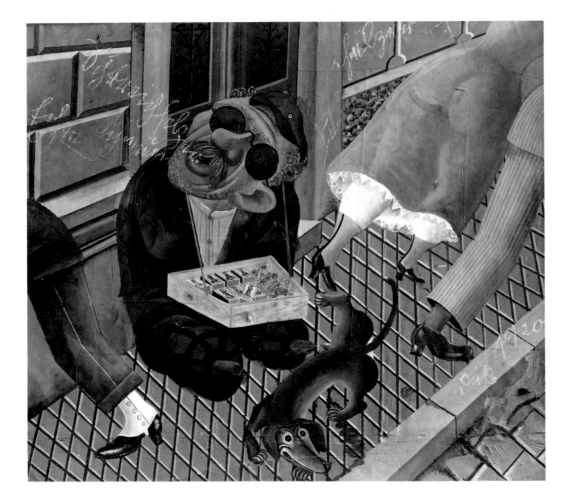

42. Otto Dix

THE MATCH SELLER

1920. Oil on canvas, 55¾ × 65⅜″. Staatsgalerie, Stuttgart

1940), who, with poignant timing, was drafted into the German infantry a week after Marc's death. A survivor of the war, Klee was appointed in 1921 to the Bauhaus, whose purist dreams of Utopian reconstruction ran counter to Dix's insistence on reportorial horror. There, Klee continued to explore his own enchanted, childlike universe, which often perpetuated, though in a less philosophically ponderous vein, Marc's efforts to penetrate the psychology of animals.

When Klee turned to dogs, as he did in a painting of 1928, *She Howls, We Play (fig. 43)*, he provided the same light touch mixed with profound empathy that characterizes all his work. Here, as the title suggests (and Klee's titles are often essential clues to understanding what we see), we are cast in the unfamiliar role of three frolicking puppies whose mother, wiser than we are, is howling at some menace we couldn't care less about. Gauguin's three puppies, for all their fairy-tale simplicity *(fig. 37)*, seem positively earthbound next to Klee's linear wraiths, a finely knotted tangle of childish doodles that conveys the mindless activity of this carefree trio. By contrast, their (or our) mother is taut, nervous, alert, instantly protecting her brood by howling at a danger further evoked by the stains of red that pulsate here and there in Klee's magically vibrant ground of disembodied color. All the visual means here, as well as the imaginative ones, hark back to our childhood memories of our discovery of line and color, of our assumptions of adult watchfulness and infant play, a miraculous regression that, typically for Klee and, indeed, for many other artists of the interwar period, suggests that the deepest realities, if we can reach them, belong to the domain of instinct, even of dreams and nightmares.

It was a revelation explored both independently and communally after the war, and nowhere with more programmatic focus than by the Surrealists, who established their group identity with a manifesto in 1924. In their sophisticated search for the elemental stuff of which the id is said to be made, few were so successful as the Catalan master Joan Miró (1891–1983), who, in the heyday of Surrealism, often captured the primordial magic of the simplest, most indelible emotions and images. Among the best known of these works is *Dog Barking at the Moon* of 1926 *(fig. 44)*, which, like Klee's immersion into canine instinct, permits us to regress to childlike wonder and innocence. Almost a textbook example of a Freudian dream of an unattainable, infantile goal, the narrative is as plain as folklore, showing us an earthbound dog foolishly barking at a crescent man in the moon suspended in a jet black sky. At the left, this impossible leap from reality to wish fulfillment is underscored by the irrational perspective rush of a ladder to nowhere, its dizzying ascent mocked by the birdlike cloud form (as Miró himself identified it) seemingly just within reach of the highest rung. The simple meaning here seems as rooted in folk wisdom as is Runge's silhouette of a dog barking at the moon *(fig. 17)*, and the profiled clarity of these flatly colored shapes (often evoking the red-yellow, black-white palette familiar to Spain and its artists) may also recall that tradition of creating the simplest images with scissors and paper, as in Picasso's little cutout of a dog *(fig. 38)*. But for all its willful ingenuousness, Miró's silly dog strikes more sinister tones. The pitch-black sky against the deep brown earth; the spooky illumination of dog, cloud, and ladder by the milky light of an eerie man in the moon; the sense of a dog's total isolation in an unin-

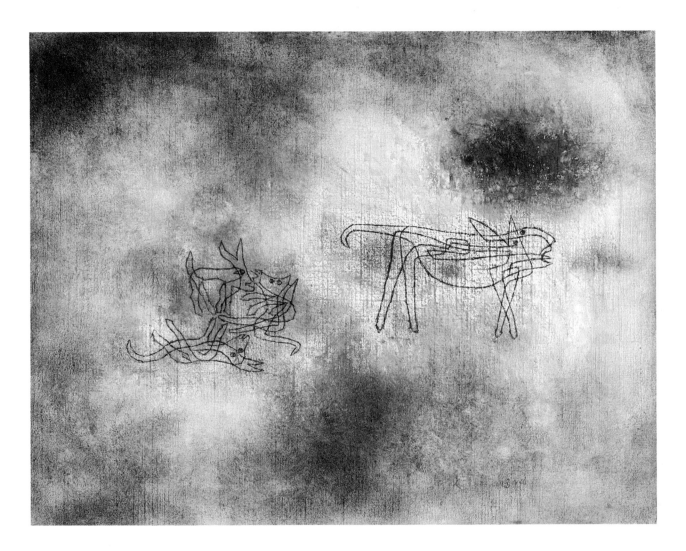

43. Paul Klee

SHE HOWLS, WE PLAY

1928. Oil on canvas, 17⅛ × 22¼″. Kunstmuseum, Bern. Paul Klee Foundation

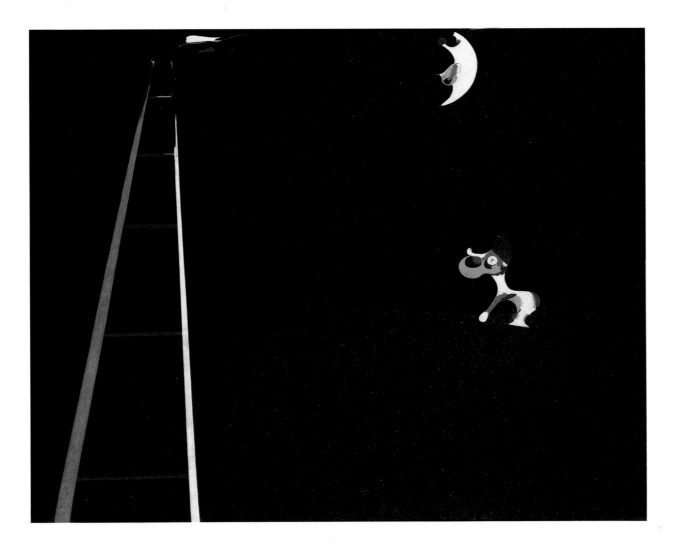

44. Joan Miró

DOG BARKING AT THE MOON

1926. Oil on canvas, 29 × 36¼″. Philadelphia Museum of Art. A. E. Gallatin Collection

habited land—such is the stuff that can turn comic proverbs into unsettling dreams, entering territory that may suddenly suggest even a general kinship with the black paintings by Miró's compatriot Goya and, within that series, a particular memory of that most nightmarish of dogs *(fig. 18)*. Like Goya, Miró often transformed childish folly into a grotesque mirror of the instincts dominating the adult world.

On more twentieth-century levels, Miró's canvas offers fascinating analogies with a modern, popular domain of free-wheeling fantasy. Miró himself referred to his preliminary drawing for the painting as "a kind of comic strip," and in that pencil sketch, in fact, he drew in comic-strip balloons containing a dialogue between dog and moon, which he then scribbled over. The dog says: "Boub boub" (French onomatopoeia for a howl). The moon answers, in nursery-like rhyme: "Je m'en fou" ("I don't give a damn"). And the first inscribed title, *Toutou jappant la lune* ("Bowwow Yapping at the Moon"), has a similarly infantile ring. As such, Miró's painting, although executed in a milieu of the most avant-garde exploration, ironically intersects a long twentieth-century tradition of popular fantasy art in both style and imagery, carrying us from such archaic moments in the history of cinema and comic strip as Méliès's *Trip to the Moon* (1904) and Herriman's *Krazy Kat* (beginning 1914) up to the technicolor world of Walt Disney in which dogs, as foolish as Miró's or as noble as Landseer's, have played, as simple-minded surrogates, every human role in a popular dramatic repertory.

Art-historical convention would contrast sharply Miró's abstract mode of Surrealism, with its flattened spaces, opaque colors, and amoeboid contours, to the quasi-photographic mode best known in the work of another Catalan painter, Salvador Dalí (1904–1989), but the gulf between them is hardly so unbridgeable. In their different languages, both artists can create a dreamscape of disquieting vastness and desolation (often at the edge of the sea) and a sense of metamorphic magic that can translate the commonplace into the hallucinatory. Such is the mystery in one of Dalí's paintings of a dog who does not even figure in the title, the *Apparition of Face and Fruit Dish on a Beach* of 1938 *(fig. 45)*. A wizard at inventing multiple images of the uninhibited kind sought out by psychiatrists working with Rorschach tests and free-association therapy, Dalí locates us here at what looks like a deserted coastal region familiar to Catalonia and to Miró's art as well. It is easy to find, as in a desert mirage, a sphinxlike face staring out at us, and then, lo and behold, to watch this be transformed into a huge fruit dish filled with almost sexually animated ripe pears. Less quickly discernible is the way the foreground wasteland turns into an almost sacramental tablecloth for the fruit dish, whose image, in turn, is repeated in Lilliputian dimensions in a remote community of tiny nomads who seem to dwell in the rubble of some sacred grottoes. But then this irrational shift in scale and identity startles us on an even more encompassing level, a huge, collared dog (head upper right, haunches upper left) in looming profile who suddenly becomes more palpable than the disappearing act he frames until we realize that his front legs, too, have vanished. Dalí, it should be recalled, admired Gérôme's little terrier *(fig. 36)*, and was happy to perpetuate the hyper-realist techniques of French academicians which to him were so obsessively real that, like Alice peering into the looking glass, they crossed the border of the irrational. As in those elusive dreams that Freud and the Surrealists believed could reveal our deepest truths, this colossal dog surfaces and disappears, congeals and evaporates before our eyes. And just as we feel we can touch its living head, we realize that its eye sockets are completely hollow, offering a telescopic view of a landscape as inaccessibly remote as the moon Miró's dog barks at. Flesh and fur have become bone; the dog has turned into a fossil. Private though this fantasy may seem, the painting's date, 1938, tells us, as do many other works of the late 1930s by Dalí, Miró, and Picasso, about the specter of war, not only the civil war raging in Spain, but the one so soon to come. The mood is of apocalyptic devastation and primitive survival in a prehistoric landscape, a vision of modern warfare that Spanish masters, as far back as Goya, translated into pictorial nightmares.

This sense of horrifying regression and bleakness penetrated many other canine images created during and just after the Second World War. So it is in another fierce canvas, *Dog Howling at the Moon* (*fig. 46*), painted in 1943 by the Mexican Rufino Tamayo (b. 1899). Although in the 1930s Tamayo was mainly attracted to picturesque, folkloric images of Mexican markets, carnivals, and peasants, the mood of his art blackened in the 1940s when he divided his time between Mexico City and New York. His howling dog, painted the year following Mexico's official declaration of war on the Axis powers, is as apocalyptic in tone as any of its ancestors in the European version of the Hispanic tradition. A canine colossus, this dog seems to have reverted, like mankind, to its original savage instincts. The *Guernica*-like door at the right, and the manmade bowl, filled with dry bones, suggest the former

presence of a caring human master who has long since vanished or perhaps has even been devoured, leaving the animal howling wildly, with bared white teeth, against an intensely blue night sky. The strange crescent moon itself evokes cataclysm, for it presents an eclipse familiar in the apocalyptic symbolism of the Catholic art so ingrained in the Hispanic tradition. Tamayo's metaphor of a domesticated animal transformed into a lone and brutal predator brings into the war years an image that seems to recur on the soil of Spain and Latin America.

In Northern Europe as well, the wartime shadow of terror and loneliness fell across the art of the 1940s and early 1950s, leaving at least two images of dogs so haunting that they have become part of the canon of twentieth-century art. The first is a bronze of 1951, only eighteen inches high, by the Swiss artist Alberto Giacometti (1901–1966) that turns the nineteenth-century tradition of decorative bronze dog sculpture inside out (*fig. 47*). Completely at one with both the form and the feeling of that strange race of ascetically thin, almost impalpable people Giacometti began to create during the war years, this dog also appears to be an urban dweller, a lonely scavenger in Paris, the heir to Seurat's black mongrel (*fig. 30*). Quite unlike the bronze of his brother Diego's cat that Giacometti sculpted in the same year, a completely impersonal example of feline grace, this dog looks like an individual, its long, emaciated muzzle and drooping neck distinctive as it walks across some urban thoroughfare. Luckily, we have the artist's own words to reinforce such intuitions: "For a long time I'd had in my mind the memory of a Chinese dog I'd seen somewhere. And then one day I was walking along the rue de Vanves

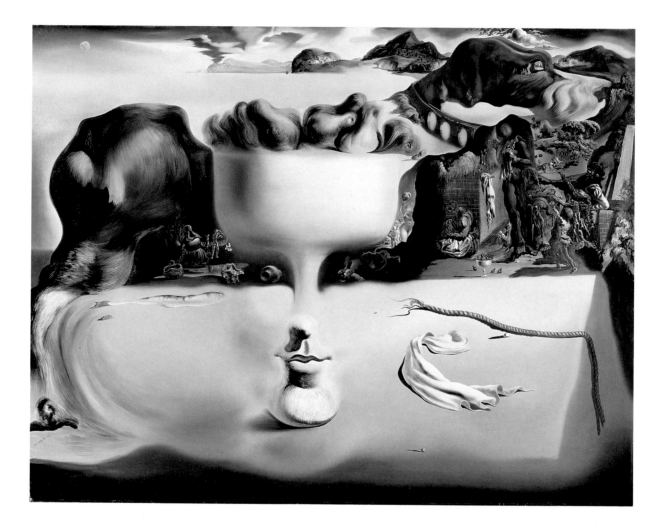

45. Salvador Dalí

APPARITION OF FACE AND FRUIT DISH ON A BEACH

1938. Oil on canvas, 45 × 56⅝″. Wadsworth Atheneum, Hartford.

The Ella Gallup Sumner and Mary Catlin Sumner Collection

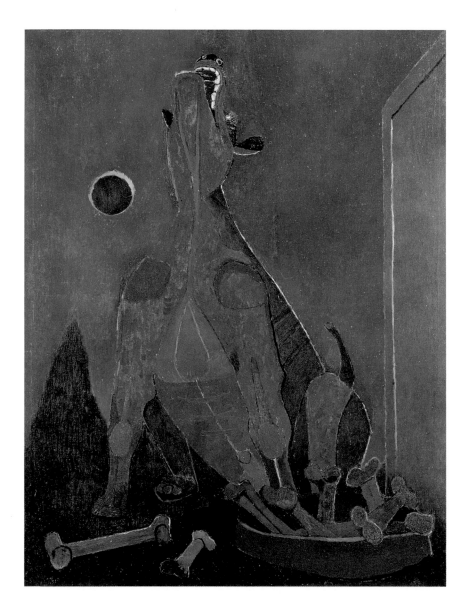

46. Rufino Tamayo

DOG HOWLING AT THE MOON

1943. Oil on canvas, 47¼ × 33½". Private collection

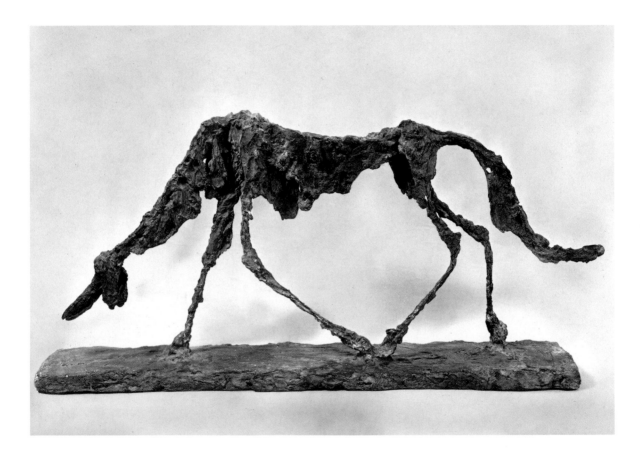

47. *Alberto Giacometti*

D O G

1951. Bronze (cast 1957), height 18″, base 39 × 6⅛″. Collection The Museum of Modern Art, New York.

A. Conger Goodyear Fund

in the rain, close to the walls of the buildings, with my head down, feeling a little sad, perhaps, and I felt like a dog just then. So I made that sculpture." No less than Giacometti's human population of totally isolated figures, eroded to the very core of some living nerve tissue that firmly proclaims their emotional presence, his dog belongs to that postwar Parisian ambience familiarly called Existentialism, with its sense of desperately lonely, sentient, and proud human beings set adrift in an uncaring universe. Giacometti's *Dog* might well have belonged to Jean-Paul Sartre. Its connection with celebrities, however, was not only metaphorical but real; for in the late 1950s, a visitor to the Museum of Modern Art in New York named Marlene Dietrich saw this bronze dog, and was so smitten by it that she decided, on her next trip to Paris in late 1959, to make it her business to meet Giacometti. In fact she did, befriending him for a short period and receiving, in homage, a small plaster—of a human being, however, not a dog.

The existential loneliness of Giacometti's Parisian dog has a major rival across the English channel in a series of dog paintings also executed in the early 1950s by Francis Bacon (b. 1909). The image he chose of a large mastiff approaching us from an angle was inspired, like so many of Bacon's themes, by a photograph, in this case of the very dog, Dread (the most apt of names for Bacon!), who had posed for Muybridge's serial photographs of the mid-1880s *(fig. 25)*. Choosing frame #9 in which the dog's head was blurred in a ghostly way, Bacon then relocated the animal in a series of different locales— Monte Carlo, the Nazi stadium at Nuremberg, and in the last of the group, dated 1953 *(fig. 48)*, what appears to be the most fogbound and gloomy of Lon-

don streets, viewed against nocturnal blackness and eerie lamplight. In this version, the phantom isolation of the dog is made still more uncanny by the presence (or non-presence) of the lower half of a shadowy master who holds the animal by an equally immaterial leash. The visual souvenirs here hark back not only to Muybridge, but also to the Futurists, for Balla's *Leash in Motion (fig. 41)* hovers like a specter, although a most cheerful one, over this image of a pedestrian spook and his ectoplasmic dog. And the suggestion of measured regularity in the pavement stones and sewer grate further intensifies the contrast between the vestiges of a rational, manmade environment and the translucent smudges that mark within it the ephemeral passage of formerly solid, living things, a nightmarish vision whose potential was all too real after Hiroshima.

For the vast postwar audiences who did not want to be reminded of existential isolation or new ways of disintegrating the flesh of man and beast, there were many artists who could nostalgically recall a more secure world in which things were what they seemed and in which old-fashioned values still prevailed. Two such popular masters of the same generation emerged in the 1940s on both sides of the U.S.-Canadian border, Andrew Wyeth (b. 1917) and Alex Colville (b. 1920). As for Wyeth, his life and art give the appearance of shutting the door on the twentieth century and throwing away all keys except those to public success. Limiting himself to the record of the life he knows in the most rural, backwater territories of Pennsylvania and Maine, Wyeth mirrors the survival of some archaic pioneer spirit in North America, where people and their dogs are at one with the hardships of living close to a nature that is seldom benevolent. Here, the population is so

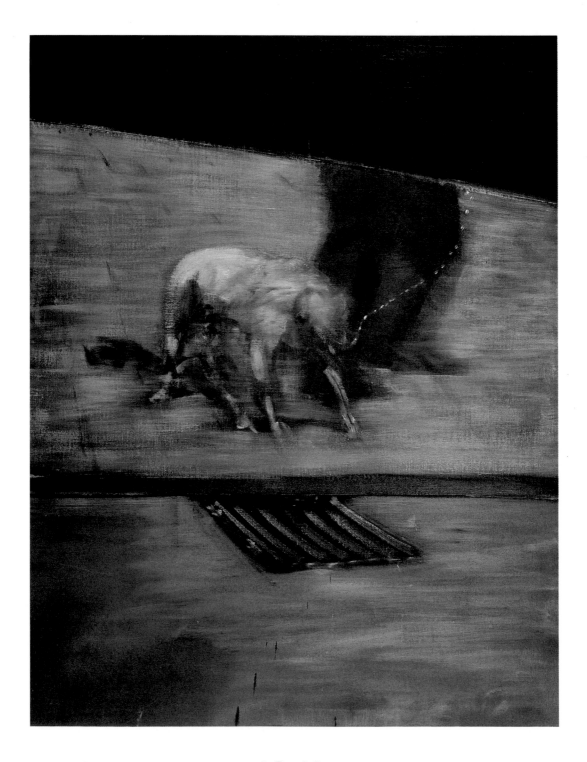

48. Francis Bacon

MAN WITH DOG

1953. Oil on canvas, 60×46″. Albright-Knox Art Gallery, Buffalo. Gift of Seymour H. Knox, 1955

small that dogs, like people, tend to appear alone, the only specimen for miles; and here, such solitude apparently toughens character rather than raising European-style existential questions about facing the void. Wyeth's dogs provide companionship for a dweller in an old wooden house or, as in *After the Chase*, a watercolor of 1965 *(fig. 49)*, they hunt for food for their masters, an archaic occupation rarely depicted in the more experimental art of our century. A lone Yankee descendant of the aristocratic packs of hunting dogs depicted in British and French eighteenth-century art, and still at work in Troyon's pointer *(fig. 22)*, Wyeth's hound, sturdy but still panting after the chase, is an image of fidelity, of hard work, and of the moral fiber needed for simple survival in the country. Almost rooted to the secure young tree (contrasted to the old dead one that has been felled in the background), he takes his steadfast place below a high-gabled rural dwelling, as much a part of the landscape as he is. This praise of the rigorous old ethic of a remote, pre-industrial America is matched by the forthright, no-nonsense craft of Wyeth, the sworn realist, who here, even in the more liquid medium of watercolor, will dot every "i" and cross every "t," from the tiniest of petals to the most intricate of bark grain. And the colors, too, with their restriction to earthy grays, browns, beiges conjure up a rugged asceticism that would reject any lure of the sensuous or artificial.

The popularity of such myths about the survival, in the postwar world, of pre-war, grass-roots North American life is matched north of the border in Colville's work. Born in Toronto, but raised in Nova Scotia, just northeast of Wyeth's equally bleak and craggy Maine, Colville might be described as Canada's answer to Wyeth, sharing both his overwhelm-ing popular success and his nostalgia for so many values trampled under in the postwar world. It is no surprise that Colville, too, resurrects the hunting dog at work. In *Hound in a Field* of 1958 *(fig. 50)*, we are transported to a Canadian version of Wyeth country, where the air is clear and pure, and the landscape, with its bleached-out patches of late autumnal grass and early snow, alien to the comforts as well as the troubles of an urban world that seems light-years away. The sole protagonist is a hunting dog, whom we scrutinize close-up on its own turf with the startling intimacy of a dog's vision as well as a dog's sense of smell. For this hound has just made an abrupt but elegantly poised turn, and we share its sudden excitement as it scents in the opposite direction the presence of, most likely, a rabbit, just as we share with Troyon's French country dog *(fig. 22)* the thrill of the chase in an open field. Like Wyeth, Colville revives an almost Pre-Raphaelite exactitude of detail, whose sharp, hair-by-hair and weed-by-weed focus is emphasized by the use of casein tempera, a medium that creates dry, finely brushed surfaces contributing to this ascetic labor and clarity; and like Wyeth, Colville extols a North American neo-Puritanism, not only in the anti-sensuous color of the coming of a rigorous winter, but in the feeling of strength through solitude, here underlined by the distant but looming infinity of the wilderness, its evergreens and now leafless trees suggesting the enduring cycles of nature.

But there are very real dogs in nature, even in Maine, who can startle us with a shock of modernity that turns Wyeth's and Colville's hounds into nostalgic anachronisms. Such is the case with *Sunny #4* *(fig. 51)*, a huge canvas of 1971 by the New York artist Alex Katz (b. 1927). Everything about it,

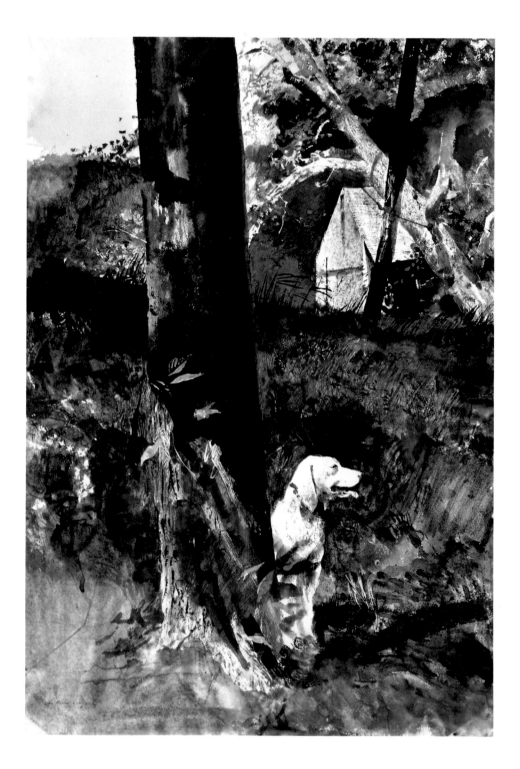

49. Andrew Wyeth

AFTER THE CHASE

1965. Watercolor on paper, 29⅛ × 19⅛″. Collection Wichita Art Museum, Kansas

whether its unusually large dimensions (some eight feet high), its arresting, head-on confrontation, or its colossal scale, packs the most unsentimental of wallops, especially given the fact that the breed, a Skye terrier, being ground-hugging, seldom looms over horizons and that this particular dog, being the artist's beloved family pet, was more accustomed to the domestic fondling of the New York lapdog than the rigors of the great outdoors. Undermining the modestly scaled tradition of frontal dog portraits, Sunny seems infinitely bigger than life, making us feel like a rabbit who suddenly looked up to find a panting dog at alarmingly close range. His size, in fact, increases at a breathless pace as we realize that the two alert ears, like TV antennae, extend so far outward they are cropped by the canvas edges and that between this awesome span, they encompass a sweeping horizon that cuts across a distant green forest and the deepest blue waters, telescoping a setting at Dutch Trap Cove near the artist's summer home in Lincolnville, Maine.

This Brobdingnagian scale, typical of Katz's human portraits, is far closer to public than to private fantasy, relating as it does to the crazy gigantism of American popular imagery, from cinema screens to Times Square billboards, visual media that left their huge imprint on the scale and bold simplifications of Katz's work. Within this breadth, which also conveys the heroic expanses of the Abstract Expressionist canvases that were part of Katz's visual milieu, Sunny is nevertheless the most particularized and pettable of dogs, with every strand of his centrally parted, furry mask as itemized as the weeds that half-conceal him, and with an especially beguiling contrast between exposed pink tongue and concealed dark eyes.

Another kind of modernity, as reportorial as it is visual, can be found in the uncanny sculpture of Duane Hanson (b. 1925), whose far more than reasonable facsimiles of the lower social strata of America, from bums and unskilled workers to the patrons of cut-rate shopping centers, have constantly stopped art audiences in their tracks. When dogs appear, they are given equal time with their mistresses as social documents; and even alone, as in *Beagle in a Basket* of 1981 *(fig. 52)*, they can pinpoint as well as any photograph a cluster of ugly and unhappy facts about American life. As disconcertingly indolent, overfed, and alone as most of the lower-middle-class people who inhabit Hanson's world of redneck interiors, this pet beagle also captures, in an exact clone of reality, the kind of documentary truth familiar to photography and to the so-called Photo-Realist painters who recorded the American scene. Here, the dog's minimal domestic environment— the rectangle of shag rug and the imitation wicker basket—tells as much about an entire cross section of American life and taste as the dime-store accessories in Hanson's figure sculpture. But the effect of this eerie replication of animate as well as inanimate objects goes beyond both sociology and taxidermy into an eternally immobilized world where art, life, and death are morbidly fused. Like the dogs of A.D. 79 who lived in the shadow of Vesuvius and were suddenly preserved forever in the volcanic ashes that killed them and their human companions, Hanson's lazy little beagle paralyzes a living moment in history that can speak volumes about American pet dogs and their owners in A.D. 1981. And it may come as no surprise to learn that this particular dog was, in fact, the Hanson family pet, Petra, metamorphosed after her sudden death into her own funerary effigy.

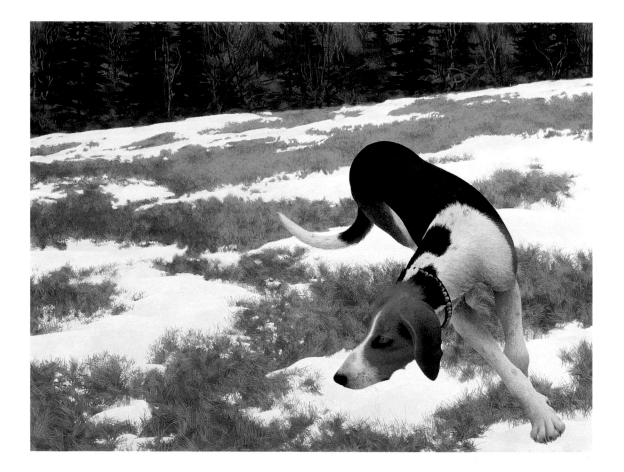

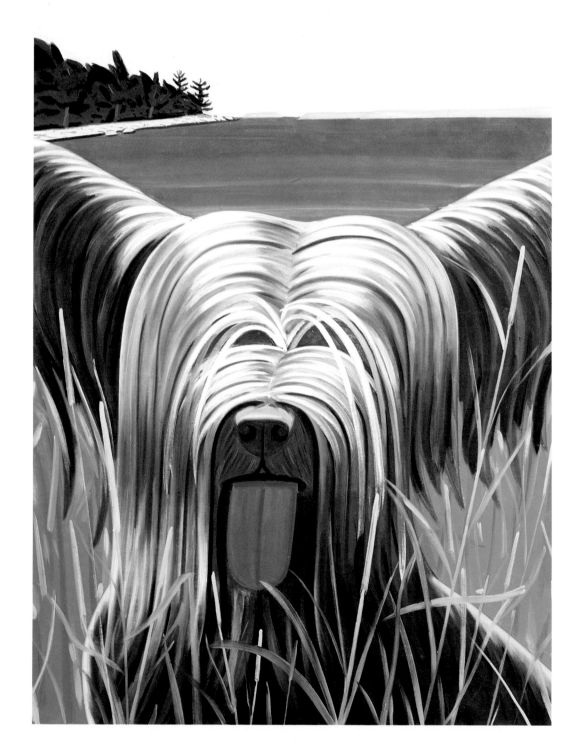

51. Alex Katz

SUNNY #4

1971. Oil on canvas, 96 × 72″. Milwaukee Art Museum Collection. Gift of Mrs. Harry Lynde Bradley

Hanson's practice of art as duplication was shared on multiple levels by many of his contemporaries who, like Hanson, were fascinated by the wholesale intrusion of the most prosaic and ugly American realities into the domain of high art and by the possibilities of replicating not living dogs and people but their visual environment of popular imagery, as reproduced in belt-line multiples. The lightest, most ironic touch of these Pop artists is wielded by Roy Lichtenstein (b. 1923), who forced into the ivory-tower spaces of galleries and museums the kind of populist repertory of cheap illustration and emotion Hanson's sitters might feel at home with.

Lichtenstein's dogs are as preposterously caricatural as his people, doing exactly what dogs in comic strips and cartoons are supposed to do, but even more so. *Grrr!*, a big painting of 1965 *(fig. 53)*, is the archetypal vicious dog, the sort that would play a canine villain as mean as its human counterpart, the campily evil Cruella in Walt Disney's *101 Dalmatians*, released in 1961, when Lichtenstein, like Warhol, was beginning to draw and to paint cartoon characters. Pulling out all stops in the comic strip repertory, Lichtenstein turns the popular myth of loyal, benevolent Fido on its head, confronting us instead with an overscaled monster. Looming high above the horizon on a desert plane, he stares us down eyeball to eyeball, and makes his threat even clearer by the extravagance of the caption, which spells his harrowing growl with eleven R's and two exclamation points. And the magnification of benday dots and of the coarsest of printer's-ink contours to heroic dimensions adds to this affectionate scrutiny and spoof of the visual and emotional language that communicates most bluntly to American popular audiences.

As for Andy Warhol (1928–1987), who began to explore comic-strip imagery at the same time as Lichtenstein, but then moved quickly to the reproduction of another kind of reproduction, photography, dogs play a minor but acutely personal role. In the 1970s, when Warhol moved up the social ladder in art and life from cheap tabloids and superstar-gazing to a stellar role of his own in the international jet set, he painted one by one a vast anthology of the glamorous and wealthy characters who populated this world, from New York art moguls to Japanese businessmen and French designers. Within this Who's Who, in which silkscreen photographs of the sitters are fused with the bravura paint handling associated with a tradition of society portraiture, there suddenly appear, in 1976, a few canine faces, including one of Warhol's own pets, a pair of miniature dachshunds named Archie and Amos *(fig. 54)*. It is Amos who gets the same royal treatment as Warhol's human celebrities, recorded in candid head shots as if by the flashbulb of a news photographer on the run. But Amos's image is also overlaid with phantom shadows, doubled contours, and synthetic color tints that produce a haunting, almost Baconesque afterimage. Given Warhol's studied emotional detachment from people, it may be wrong to intuit from such a canine portrait a more personal involvement with the sitter; but Warhol lore at least includes the information that Amos and Archie were the artist's intimate companions and, in the words of John Richardson, "the only living things to share his bed." Emotional biography aside, Warhol's dog portraits revive, no less than his human portraits of the 1970s, what might have seemed a moribund tradition of society portraiture, in which people and their pets are presented with a calculated nonchalance, tokens of easy elegance chosen from candid snapshots and then embellished, as by clothing or cosmetics, with a rapid, virtuoso brushwork.

Unlike Warhol's pet dachshunds, who, kept private in their master's life, make only a sneak appearance in his art, Man Ray (1970–1982), the pet weimaraner of William Wegman (b. 1942), was both a public celebrity and the subject of photographic impersonations alternately poignant and hilarious. A more arty and sophisticated successor to such famous movie canines as Rin Tin Tin (1920s), Asta (1930s), and Lassie (1940s), Man Ray even made television appearances both in person and with his videotapes on such network talk shows as "The Tonight Show" and "Late Night with David Letterman." Paralleling the photographic self-portraits by Cindy Sherman, in which she plays one stereotyped role after another in a complete fiction that includes clothing, wig, makeup, and set change, Man Ray, as directed by his loyal master Wegman, performs for the camera one charade after another—dressed like Louis XIV; dusted with talc like a human baby; finding solitude in a canoe; or tucked in bed with his dog wife watching late-night television. To these revivals of a long popular tradition of canine capers, in which dogs play human roles, there are also more up-to-date art-historical references that live up to the dog's own name, Man Ray.

Blue Period of 1981 *(fig. 55)* is one of these. Here, the ever-patient Man Ray re-creates, with variations, one of modern art's most famous icons of ascetic solitude, Picasso's very old and very blue guitarist of 1903, which is presented as a reproduction in a dime-store frame. The guitar itself springs to life as Man Ray's major accessory, but the old musician's almost skeletal crossed legs are also trans-

formed into a single blue bone that wittily suggests both mortality and dinner. And as a final appropriation on this all-blue ground, the guitarist's melancholy face, modeled in ghostly blue, is mimicked by Man Ray, who affects emotions so deeply depressing that the pervasive blue mood can actually be seen as a specter on his muzzle. And at the risk of overburdening the delectably light touch of this canine recreation of a Picasso, it should also be said that Wegman's borrowings from other works of art, past and present (which, in fact, increased in his later portraits of Fay Ray, Man Ray's female successor to the artist's affections and camera lens), were symptoms of a pervasive condition in the art of the 1970s and 80s that, for want of a better word, we call Post-Modernism. On this level and on far more pretentious ones, the ghost of the art-historical past looms larger and larger as artists, like the rest of us, realize that the progressive, optimistic thrust of Modernism has long ago expired, and that it is far easier now to face backward than forward to what hardly looks any longer like the Utopian future once envisioned by Modernist generations. The key prefixes these days seem to be "neo" and "retro," historicizing attitudes that have been creating the most diverse anthology of Post-Modernist dogs.

Hardly as "human" as Man Ray and infinitely more sinister as a canine performer is another unique dog, this time painted rather than photographed, who acts out the strange mysteries dreamed up by Ed McGowin (b. 1938). Since 1974, McGowin has fixed on an eerily luminous and seemingly hairless variation on a bullterrier as the sole protagonist for an ongoing series of what might be thought of as neo-Surrealist situations. Here we feel the ghost of Magritte, whose sharp-focus depiction

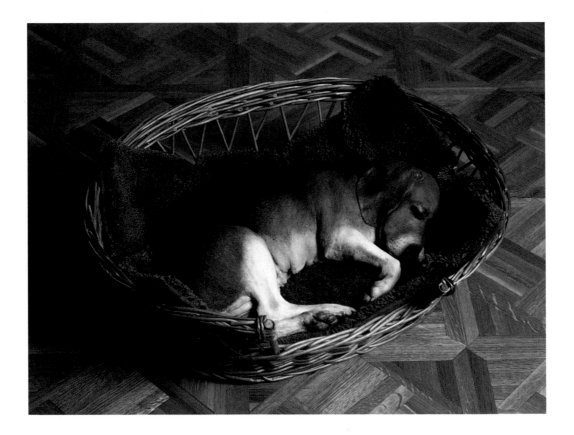

52. *Duane Hanson*

BEAGLE IN A BASKET

1981. Polyvinyl, polychromed in oil, with accessories, lifesize. Collection the artist

of the prosaic turned into the fantastic is revived not only in terms of McGowin's preference for domestic interiors but by his airbrush technique that suggests the documented reality of photography. In *Triptych* of 1986 *(fig. 58)*, the immaculate, dustless corner of a room is seen at a dog's-eye level, a homey periphery of polished floor boards, white dado, and blue wall that would seem inconsequential in the human scheme of things were it not enclosing a startlingly demonic canine presence. Confronting us with one diabolic eye and a threatening grin, this low-lying dog radiates an ominous, supernatural aura, as if Satan himself were making an unexpected appearance in canine guise. Within a worldly American interior, this otherworldly spookiness, worthy of a Steven Spielberg movie, is further enforced by the odd debris of roses on the floor, evoking both a brutal scuffle and an offering to a holy shrine, a religious association that swells to neo-Gothic dimensions in the large gilded triptych frame (which may be opened or closed and is covered with objects from a lady's boudoir) that would sanctify this creature who may have come from hell or, more likely, from the darker side of the artist's imagination. As McGowin himself has claimed, "I've identified with the dog psychologically in a way I don't understand at all. It's become part human."

The medieval revival suggested by McGowin's use of a triptych was used for totally different ends by the photographer Neil Winokur (b. 1945), who has made portraits of both people and dogs in an unexpected format familiar to Christian art: a central image, as of a saint or of Christ himself, with side panels offering attributes or related narrative events. In the case of Winokur's human portraits, the sitters are enshrined presences, accompanied by side panels that document single objects—a favorite book, a token of a hobby—which symbolize some aspect of the person's life, much as a wheel might signify St. Catherine or a lion, St. Jerome. And quite the same format and conception could be used when the sitter is a dog, as in the 1986 triptych portrait of *Nero (fig. 59)*, a shiny black pug who, incidentally, shares his name with the pet dog of Napoleon III's son, the Prince Imperial (sculpted with his Nero by Carpeaux in 1866–67), but who seems to deserve it more, given his color and Roman imperial expression. To the left and right of the sitter are two attributes, favorite chewy rubber toys in the form of a lamb chop and a lady's foot, both of whose red calligraphic accents elegantly match Nero's thin collar while offering a trickle of animation against the grounds of solid color rectangles that Winokur uses as a foil to his sitters and their attributes. Reminiscent of the hard-edged planes of opaque color familiar to a tradition of abstract geometric painting, this background also recalls the gold environments used in medieval art to evoke an immaterial, eternal space. What might be the most prosaic of dog photographs, a miniature pet with its miniature toys, turns into something surprisingly timeless and symbolic, fixing in symmetry the sitter and the almost sacred relics of his canine world.

It was, in fact, this more emblematic, one might even say hieroglyphic aspect of reinventing primary images that began to surface in canine, as well as human iconography of the 1970s and 80s, even in the domain of architecture. As for this, a particularly zany example, with a pedigree both elite and populist, is found in the work of the Chicago-based architect, Stanley Tigerman (b. 1930), who, like so many Post-Modernist artists, could seek inspiration in the

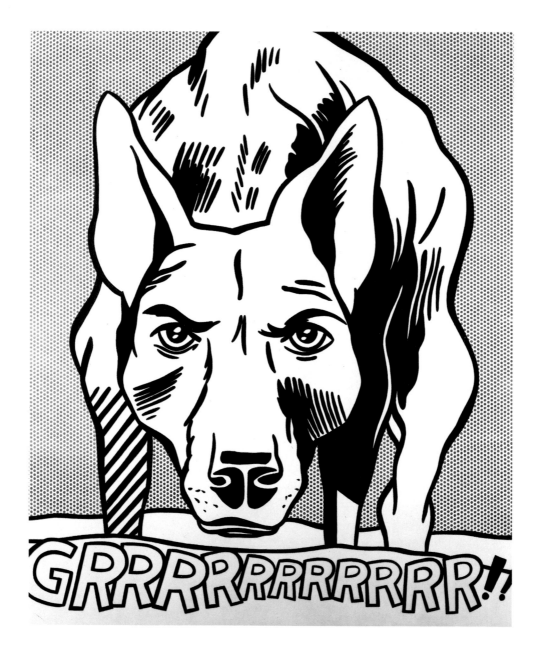

53. *Roy Lichtenstein*

GRRR!

1965. Oil and magna on canvas. 68 × 56″. Private collection

most diverse range of historical sources, quoting them with a cool and witty touch. In 1981, Tigerman redesigned a 1933 building of little character as an annex to the Anti-Cruelty Society Building in Chicago, a commission that let his Post-Modernist imagination run rampant *(fig. 56)*. The drawing-board symmetry of the pedimented facade with its regular fenestration recalls a low-budget materialization of a villa front in a Palladian pattern book; but the entrance itself suddenly proclaims another, more oddball ancestry. Appropriate to the function of the building, a modern descendant of London's RSPCA, the central image is of a dog and its attributes, or as Tigerman put it, "the cheeks of a basset hound and a key to a can of dog food," an architectural equivalent, one might say, of the invented dictionary of images in Winokur's photoportrait of *Nero*. Indeed, the pedestrian is confronted here with a neo-Surrealist double-image almost worthy of Dalí's *(fig. 45)*, as the planar ghost of a huge dog's head emerges from the gable, lunette, double door, and the profile surrounds. In effect, one enters the building through what now looks like a dog's toothy mouth under the rounded orifice of its nose. Mixing a Palladian design with both the American vernacular roadside tradition of Pop architecture (drive-in, duck-shaped diners, etc.) and the French eighteenth-century theoretical explorations of *architecture parlante* (that is, architecture that would proclaim its function by its form, such as Ledoux's notorious brothel with a ground plan in the shape of male genitals), Tigerman, like many a Post-Modernist, is happy to embrace and to juggle the whole of history and the once-clashing levels of high art and low art.

It is a position not unlike that of Keith Haring (b. 1958), who, while belonging to the sophisticated milieu of the international gallery and exhibition world, would also espouse happily the realer world out there, even descending into the New York subways as potential art territory. There he could not only practice what he preached about being a genuinely public artist, but could join the ongoing populist tradition of anonymous graffitists who, over the decades, had been adding their wild visual signatures to the drama of subway cars moving in a subterranean theater whose set designs the Metropolitan Transit Authority never dreamed of. In the early 1980s, Haring, in fact, brought his comic-strip mythology of glowing babies, kindergarten television sets, space aliens, flying angels, and not least, the most animated of dogs right into the New York subway stations, making chalk drawings, in minutes and seconds, of his instantly recognizable cartoon images on the black paper panels ephemerally visible before a new ad is pasted over them. Popping up and then swiftly disappearing on the subway platforms, as if the work of an elfin graphomaniac, hundreds of these drawings surveyed the extraterrestrial scope of Haring's sophisticatedly naive cosmos. In one at the 33rd Street Lexington Avenue station *(fig. 57)*, we see a prominent member of Haring's cast of characters, the dog, whose mythical role in his work almost demands a capital D. A popular science-fiction descendant of Miró's *Dog Barking at the Moon (fig. 44)*, this Dog is in an equally lonely universe, but one now invaded by an alien spaceship that, following the fantastic narrative of the television series *Star Trek*, is "beaming" its captive, temporarily disintegrating the body for transportation to another planet. Located like a sacrifice on top of a stepped pyramid that conjures up the most ancient

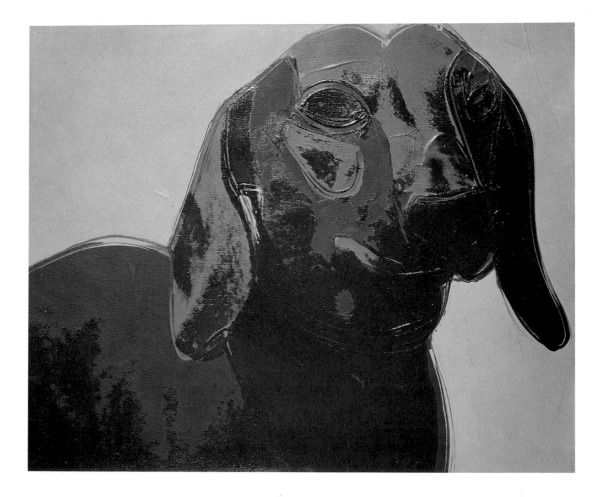

54. Andy Warhol

A M O S

1976. Oil on canvas, 25 × 32″. Estate of the artist

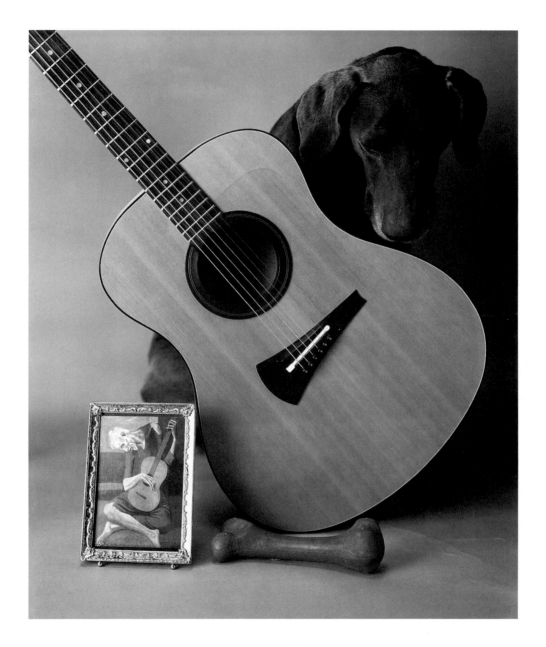

55. William Wegman
BLUE PERIOD
1981. Polacolor II, 20 × 24″. Courtesy Holly Solomon Gallery, New York

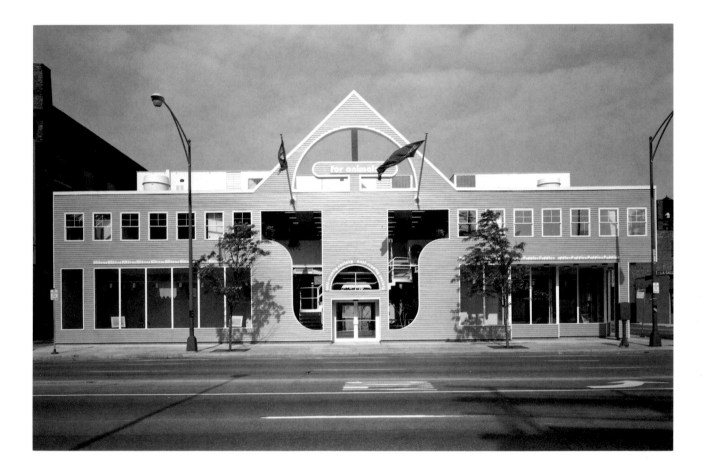

56. Stanley Tigerman

ANTI-CRUELTY SOCIETY BUILDING, CHICAGO

1981. Photograph by Howard Kaplan

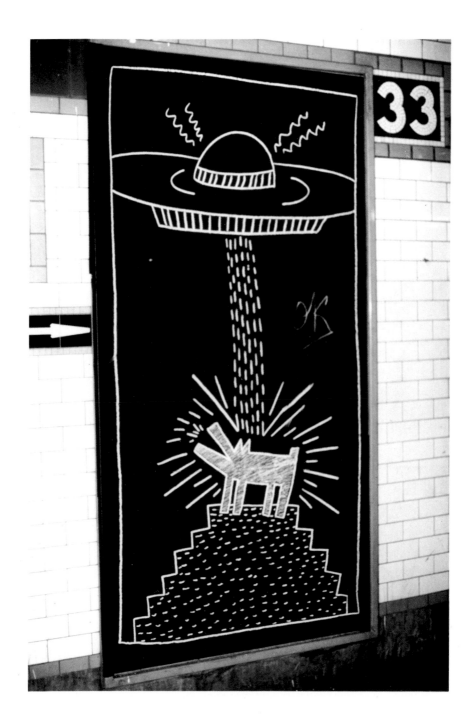

57. Keith Haring

SUBWAY GRAFFITI

c. 1983. 33rd Street, Lexington Avenue Station, New York City

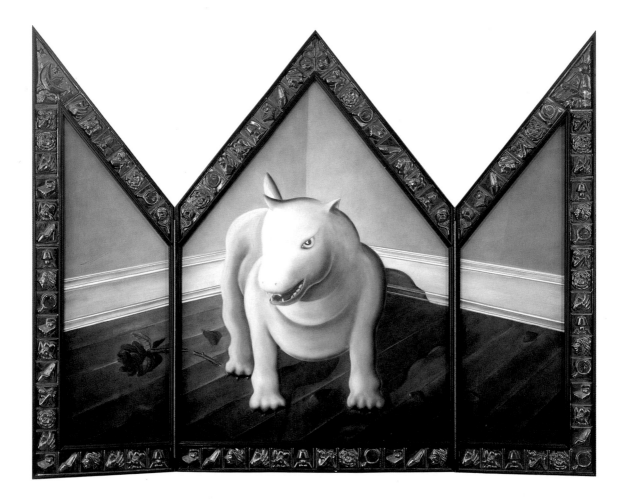

58. Ed McGowin

D O G   T R I P T Y C H

1986. Airbrush, mixed media, 60×78″. Collection David and Penny McCall, New York

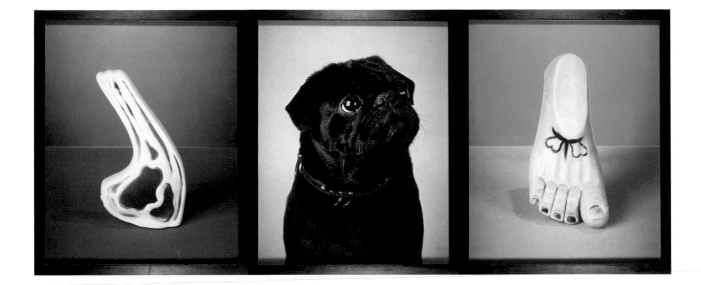

59. *Neil Winokur*

N E R O

1986. Three cibachrome photographs, 20 × 16″. Private collection, New York

temple sites of Planet Earth, the Dog is also directly below the invading UFO from an unnumbered future century, sweeping us into mythical extremes of time and space. It is a vision of another kind of apocalypse, perhaps ultimately related to Goya's and Turner's bleak views of a dog as a lone and ultimate terrestrial survivor *(figs. 18 and 19)*, but reinterpreted with the comic smile that late twentieth-century earth-dwellers often muster up nervously in the face of potentially real science-fiction fantasies about the end of the world. And on another level of time travel, Haring's Dog, a mythic message appearing on a subterranean wall below a pocket of civilization, almost offers a modern urban equivalent of the archeological magic evoked by the animal images miraculously preserved in paleolithic caves at Lascaux or Altamira. Ironically, too, the scribbled "OK" on Haring's drawing, the mark of a later, anonymous graffitist, enforces these distant memories of prehistoric cave paintings, which also disclose superimposed layers of imagery, made by one hand after another.

Haring's willingness to take his elementary vocabulary from the crude visual and narrative language of comic strips is not only a token of his wish to communicate, as these subway drawings certainly did, with a vast popular audience, but also a symptom of the many "neo" currents in recent art that reflect the retrospective, historicizing attitudes of Post-Modernism. As such his work might be seen as a kind of revival of the by now historical "ism" that was Pop Art in the early 1960s, when works like Lichtenstein's comic-strip dog *(fig. 53)* invaded the ivory towers of Art. Other artists who surfaced in the 1970s and 80s also turned to a kind of neo-Pop language that used the crudest vocabulary of cheap commercial imagery for often outrageous effect. Such is the case with Steve Gianakos (b. 1938), who revives with a vengeance the Pop artist's assaults on the aesthetic and cultural proprieties assumed to belong to the domain of high art. In one of his many dog drawings, *Ménage à Twelve* of 1976 *(fig. 60)*, Gianakos flouts just about every convention in the old elitist view of art. The dog image here is of the ABC kind, a rock-bottom geometric diagram that recalls something from a primitive how-to-draw manual for aspiring artists in Podunk or perhaps from a child's computer screen; but in Sorcerer's Apprentice fashion, it multiplies itself in delirious, belt-line quantity to reach the excesses of the sexual imagination so often released in the liberations of the 1970s. A blasphemous variation of Disney's *101 Dalmatians*, complete with black-and-white ink spots, it also offers a biological updating, in computer-world imagery, of the mechanistic dogs of Muybridge and Balla *(figs. 25 and 41)*.

Such mechanical multiplications, though of a more decorous kind, are also seen in an offbeat dog portrait by an artist generally associated with the "Neo-Geo" movement of the mid-80s, Philip Taaffe (b. 1955). In 1985, Massimo Audiello exhibited "The Chi-Chi Show" in his East Village gallery, for which a group of up-and-coming artists were invited to submit portraits of Chi-Chi, the pet chihuahua of another East Village dealer, Pat Hearn. Since Taaffe worked almost exclusively in the domain of re-creating, in a Post-Modernist way, the abstract geometric paintings that reigned in the 1950s and 60s, it was hard to predict how he would portray a miniature pet dog. But the result was pure Taaffe *(fig. 61)*. Against a painted paper background that restates the nuanced variations on red

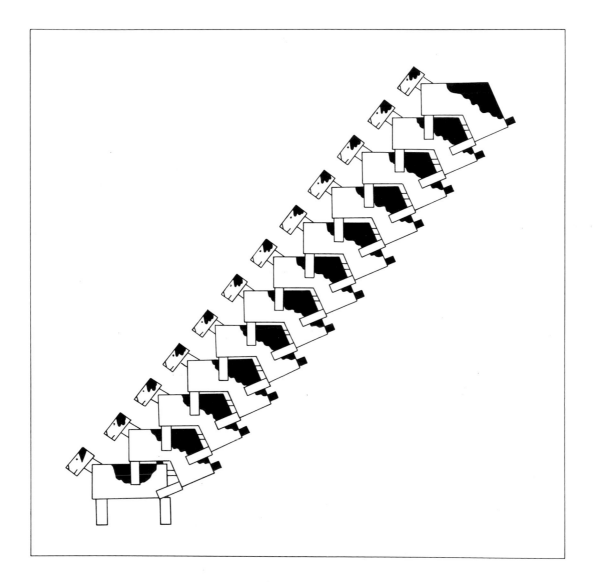

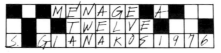

60. *Steve Gianakos*

MÉNAGE À TWELVE

1976. Ink on paper, 18×25″. Collection the artist

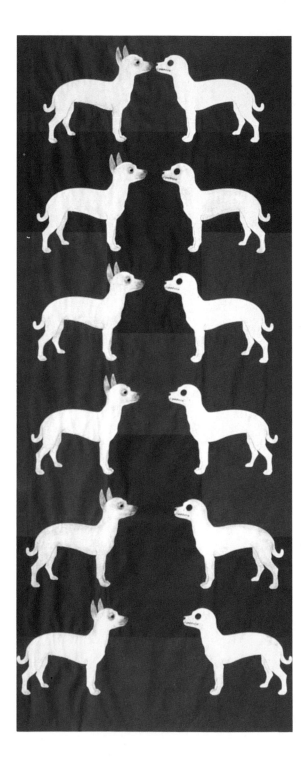

61. Philip Taaffe

CHI-CHI MEETS THE DEATH OF PAINTING

1985. Linoprint, collage, acrylic on paper, 112 × 45″. Collection Peter Brams

rectangles that Ad Reinhardt had explored in the early 1950s, Chi-Chi appears in a whimsical mixture of neo-Aztec stepped pyramid and a Muybridge-like dissection of motion in what looks like a series of frames from an animated cartoon. Facing, on the right, her mirror image as a hard-edged specter, Chi-Chi and her supernatural alter ego belong to a macabre tradition of Mexican folk art in which skeletons play living roles. But here, both she and her bony ghost ascend this geometric pyramid step by step, in perfect tandem with Reinhardt's modular background, until they finally meet, muzzle almost touching muzzle, at the top. With a cynicism typical of a younger generation confronting the void, but, like the rest of us, making hay while the sun is still shining, Taaffe titled this picture *Chi-Chi Meets the Death of Painting*. Of course, we Post-Modernists know that the death of painting has been proclaimed many times, yet painting still seems to flourish. And we may also guess that if both the human and canine races survive, dogs will continue to flourish in the future life of art.

INDEX

PHOTOGRAPH CREDITS

The author and publisher wish to thank the owners and custodians for permitting the reproduction of works of art in their collections. Photographs were generally supplied by the owners, with the notable exception of the following, designated by figure references:

Fig. 1: Service photographique de la Réunion des musées nationaux, Paris; *fig. 2:* AGRACI; *fig. 5:* Conway Library, Courtauld Institute of Art, London; *fig. 7:* Courtesy Richard L. Feigen & Co.; *fig. 11:* Musée de Poitiers (Christian Vignaud); *fig. 13:* Service photographique de la Réunion des musées nationaux, Paris; *fig. 14:* Courtesy Partridge (Fine Arts) Ltd., London; *fig. 24:* Gabinetto; *fig. 28:* Bibliothèque Nationale, cabinet des éstampes, Paris; *fig. 35:* Supplied by EMI Music, London; *fig. 38:* S.P.A.D.E.M.; *fig. 39:* Haags Gemeentemuseum, The Netherlands; *fig. 43:* © 1988, copyright COSMOPRESS, Geneva; *fig. 46:* Courtesy Mary-Anne Martin/Fine Art, New York; *fig. 49:* Henry Nelson, Wichita Art Museum; *fig. 53:* Courtesy Leo Castelli Gallery, New York; *fig. 54:* Courtesy of the Mayor Gallery, Ltd., London; *fig. 55:* Uli Koecher/Kestner-Gesellschaft, Hanover, West Germany; *fig. 56:* © HNK Architectural Photography; *fig. 57:* Tseng Swong Chi; *fig. 58:* Ken Showell; *fig. 59:* Otto Nelson; *fig. 61:* Courtesy Massimo Audiello Gallery, New York.